# Tao of Self Meaning

# Phenomenology of Healing in Art

# 道德經藝術心理學

## 中英對照

### Dr. Lau, Sze Oi. Ed.D.



ISBN:10:1725170027
ISBN-13:978-1725170025

# TO ENCOUNTERS

# CONTENTS

# ACKNOWLEDGMENTS

In 2004, I completed more than 300 pages of my thesis on "Tao, Art, and Lifelong Learning". The birth of this book is a part of my doctoral dissertation, and I also weave it together with more than 20 years of clinical experiences. The therapeutic process, like most creative processes, is messy, confusing and even ugly. Art bridges our inside and outside worlds, our fantasy and our reality.  Here, the most important issue is our "honesty."  From honesty, springs forth love, so that we can heal.   Only with an aesthetic sense can, one sees beauty in ugliness.  Only with a heart of compassion, can one touches human dignity and integrity.  Only with a mind of hope and trust, can one turns fantasy into reality.  Only with an empty spirit can, one creates something from nothing and embraces paradox.

# TAO, ART & LIFE LONG LEARNING

# I.  PART ONE

## THE TRANSFORMATION JOURNAL

Transformation is about changes: different levels and directions of change. Change depends on a view of the self, the other, and the world.  Once I saw a big billboard at O'Hara Airport while I was waiting for a flight.  On it was written, "Just push a button, it can transform your life."  Is transformation that simple?  If it is that easy in the outside world, is it as easy to do in our inside world?  A client with depression and an obsessive-compulsive disorder was sitting in my office.  She said, "I am paralyzed in front of the computer. I hate it, because I hate my parents.  I want to revenge…"  I sincerely wished that there were a button I could push, so I could instantly transform her life.  We may change the outside world by pushing a button, but we cannot change our inside world.

I will explore a process of transformation through art therapy, and Tao theories.  Lao Tzu, the philosopher seeks harmony with the universe through a communion with Tao.  The state of experiencing one's perfect union or oneness with the divine is the ultimate purpose of Tao and the outcome of meditation.  This mystic experience is the direct personal experience of ultimate self-identity, which cannot be easily shaken by change in the outside world.

## 1) PARADOX: CONSCIOUS LEARNING

It is stated in Tao Te Ching, Chapter 2 (Wing, 1986).

When the entire world knows beauty as beauty,
There is ugliness.
When they know good as good,
There is evil.
In this way
"To be" and "Not To be" arise mutually.
Difficult and easy complement each other.
Long and short contrast each other.
High and low, set measure to each other.
Pitch and tone harmonize each other.
Past and future follow each other.

Therefore, Evolved individuals
Hold their position without effort,
Practice their philosophy without words,
Are parts of all things and overlook nothing.
They produce but do not possess,
Act without expectation,
Succeed without taking credit.
Since, indeed, they take no credit.  It remains with them.

Rowley states that "The Yin and Yang relation was supposed to set up tension through the universe, between the great and the small, heaven and earth, male and female, and so on" (1955, p. 8).  At the very roots of Tao lies the principle of opposites: +ve (positive) and –ve (negative) or north and south are "different aspects of one and the same system, and the difference in the system" (Watts, 1975, p. 20).  The key to the relationship between Yin and Yang is called "hsiang sheng" (Watts, 1975, p. 21).  It means, "mutually arising.  It reflects the inseparable interconnectedness of all things" (Grigg, 1995, p. 49).

The Yin and Yang principle is not what Westerners call "dualism" (Rowley, 1955; Clarke, 2000), but rather an explicit duality expressing an implicit unity.  They are like the different, but inseparable sides of a coin, the poles of a magnet, or the pulse and interval in any vibration.  There is never the ultimate possibility that either one wins over the other.  Fortune and misfortune, life and death, whether on a small or vast scale, come and go everlastingly without beginning or end (Rowley, 1955; Cooper, 1981).

From the principle of Yin and Yang, Tao is often assumed a statement of the relativity of values.  However, beyond opposites is Tao!  Tao is absolute (Tao Te Ching, Chapter 52, Wing, 1986).   The Tao Te Ching (Chapter 2) is actually "a song of praise to the beyond-everything wholeness and absolute of Tao.  A turning away from the relative values enables us to accomplish wholeness in Tao without taking credits" (Marure, 1985, p. 2).


## 2) LEARRNING IN PARADOX: SET THE SPIRITUAL JOURNEY


> Those who know others are intelligent;
> Those who know themselves have insight;
> Those who master others have force;
> Those who master themselves have strength.
> (Tao Te Ching, Wing, 1986, Chapter 33)


In An Art of Our Own, Lipsey (1988) quotes Piet Mondrian: "The desire for freedom and equilibrium (harmony) is inherent in man (due to the universal in him).  Human beings have an inherent urge to regain the original unity of their duality" (p. 87).   According to Mondrian, the maturing inner life of a human being demonstrates the Law of "Constant contrast" to nature, and the "constant recovery of balance."  He believes that in individual history, as in world history, there is an unfolding toward unity and balance, driven by the very nature of humanness (Lipsey, 1988).


Learning takes place in contradiction: "Contradictions increase between the ways of being, understanding, behaving, and valuing which belong to yesterday and other ways of perceiving and valuing which announce the future" (Freire, 1973, p. 7). In classic Chinese, the wholeness of Tao simply means the "Way," that there is a link between what goes before and what comes after (Clarke, 2000; Cooper, 1981).  Search for the "self" is a step-by step growing experience.  The self is a process which incorporates the use of time, the intellect, emotions, experience, and reframes the pictures housed both in the conscious and unconscious realms, the museum of our personal history.  The idea is to conscious what happened.  The individual reaches different levels of awareness and knowledge, extremely personal in nature.  The process is both painful and rewarding.  Creating a new picture by experiencing self-awareness as the past and present coming together to create a whole composition might mean that one part overpowers the others.


The presence of Tao emerged from a resolution of opposites: the Yin and the Yang.  Rowley suggests that, "The fusion was a dynamic union of opposites that is the unity of life" (1955, p. 4).   Here Tao means "Self-knowledge and self-mastery are the primary Taoist accomplishments... The result is insight: the ability to perceive the larger of influences behind specific social phenomena" (Wing, 1986, Chapter 33, p. 91). In this process, it becomes crucial that the individual learns to negotiate meanings, purposes, and values critically, reflectively, and rationally instead of passively, accepting the messages defined by others.  With the Yin and Yang principle and the absolute value of Tao entering into the paradox, the road is set for personal growth and the spiritual life.


## 3) ESSENCE OF TAO: DIGNITY OF HUMAN


The Great Tao extends everywhere
It is on the left and the right
All Things depend on it for growth
In addition, it does not deny them
It achieves its purpose
In addition, it does not have a name
It clothes and cultivates All Things
In addition, it does not act as master
Always without desire

It can be named Small
All Things merge with it
In addition, it does not act as master
It can be named Great
In the end, it does not seek greatness
 And in that way the Great is achieved
(Tao Te Ching in Wing, 1986, chapter 34)


Each thing has the Tao of its particular nature, which comes from and is an aspect of the one Tao, which unites all (Tao Te Ching in Wing, 1986, Chapter 34).  Inborn nature is an inner spiritual core, which can experience fundamental unity with the Tao. "All-pervading is the Great Tao.  It can be at once on the right hand and on the left.  All things depend on it for life, and it rejects them not" (Murray, 1959, p. 22).  The Tao is a vast and unified whole, which includes all perspectives and all reality, giving all realities equal value.  "…The spiritual and the material, though we call them by different names, in their origin are one and the same.  This sameness is a mystery, -- the mystery of mysteries.  It is the gate of all wonders" (Murray, 1959, p. 20).  The Tao lets all things be; it is the space or void in which all things and perspectives find room (Tao Te Ching in Wing, 1986, Chapter 51).  "Thus it is that Tao, engendering all things, nourishes them, develops them, and fosters them; perfects them, ripens them, rends them and protects them" (Murray, 1959, p. 24).  Our real self comes from the fact that he or she makes no distinctions: "Therefore the sage does not follow such distinctions, but illuminates all in heaven" (Tao Te Ching in Wing, 1986, Chapter 5).  The real self is beyond distinctions, concepts, and labels.

Watching the patterns of life in its myriad form one can perceive everywhere a deep impulse towards transformation. In the interior of every being lies a compelling urge for change, for growth into a richer and deeper state of existence. The urge for transformation stems from a wish to be free of the sense of limitation and imperfection. This refers to a process of distinguishing the real (inner) self from the extraneous layers provided by the realm (the world and its institutions) of life (the physical self and sensory experiences which make up daily existence). Freedom does not occur by accepting the fixed limitations of one's place in the hierarchical structure of the whole, but rather by flowing with changes, assuming new perspectives, identifying this with that, and freeing one's imagination and mind from the whole of the part (Wing, 1986).

A human suffers only because he/she is ignorant of his/her true being which "is false to the Way, false to the nature and false to the nature of humanness" (Maurer, 1985, p. 21). Maurer reflects on, "People who sought to control things by knowing their secret names and by intoning the names under proper conditions. They attempt to control reality by naming it – or by having a special vocabulary for describing it" (p. 29). This is so unappealing to Lao-tzu,

The Tao of Absolute has no name.
Although infinitesimal in its Simplicity,
The world cannot master it.
Names emerge when institutions begin.
When names emerge, know likewise to stop.
To know when to stop is to be free of danger.
(Tao Te Ching in Wing, 1986, Chapter 32)

Hegemony, naming and labeling is something that screws into people's minds and hinders seeing connections. For example, I have felt fragmented and degradation since I came to North America. Human is not defined by a person, but by gender, color, and sex orientation. It is understood that we need names for the sake of learning. Once learned, we need to unlearn it and be careful of using labels to stereotype human beings. Lao-tzu seeks freedom from the restrictions and conventions of the socialized self, from social labels and external expectations. Yet, this does not mean that Taoism renounces or leaves the world. The freedom of Taoism, likewise, cannot be legislated or institutionalized; it is quite unlike the rights and liberties of Western individualism (Cleary, 1991; Clarke, 2000). Tao reminds us that one can be committed to freedom and the dignity of individuals without accepting these other forms of individualism. A human being has a body, but also a mind, spirit, and a unique capability to transcend our limitations (Clarke, 2000, pp. 90-111).

## 4) TAO AND CHANGE IN CRISIS

Tao is a dynamic change (Tao Te Ching in Wing, 1986, Chapter 25). It was said of Tao: "Being great, it passes on; passing on, it becomes remote; having become remote, it returns…" (Tao Te Ching, Chapter 25). Life on our earth is about changing. In fact, you are alive because you are changing continually and change always contains death and rebirth in every organ and

muscle of your body.  This cycle of destruction before creation is present in our physical universe.
The seed must die before a plant can emerge, "When the seasons come and go, all things die and
are reborn" (Rowley, 1955, p. 5).  It is a simple principle that even a child can draw the changes in
nature.  However, it is a lot more challenging when you are talking about your own life.  As
human beings, we cherish the familiar.  We are frightened to change – it robs us of the safety we
are accustomed to and plunges us into emotional freefell.  Most of the participants fall into this
stage, while they are in the acculturation process.

This is our dilemma – for as sure as the earth continues to turn, change will come.  In
addition, it will always come in the form of loss or in crisis.  Crisis forces us to pay attention to
our life, to our relationships, and to ourselves.  It acts like a high-powered spotlight that focuses
on you in a stage.  And it is in those moments of powerful self-reflection and personal revelation
that our real self emerges (Merton, 1962).   From the womb of darkness, each day the dawn
emerges. When we are faced with crisis or trauma, the pain is so great that the usual filters that
numb us to our emotions do not work.  It is impossible to be distracted from what is going on
inside of us.  We are forced feel everything.  It forces you to tap into reserves of courage, faith,
hope and love you were not aware you possessed.

A Chinese idiom says: "Surfing with the current wind, and break the waves."  Surfing
means learning to ride the waves, to move in the direction the current is taking us.  And that is the
best method I have discovered for dealing with pain and crisis – to move deeper into it, rather
than away from it; to surrender to our pain, rather than resist it; to dance with our pain, rather
than distance it.  Learning to dance with our pain means, it means not avoiding our feelings of
discomfort or fear; but choosing instead to consciously explore them.  It means talking about the
very thing we would rather forget.  It means giving us the time and space to indulge in sadness or
grief (Lord, 1987; Lobel, 1984).

One of the participants, Tin-en, a 40-year-old single woman, she has been taking
medication for twenty years.  She explained to me:

> *The pain was so intensive that it made me suffocate.  For several days I fought with the overwhelming
> pains and terror I felt.  I was alone; the pain was unbearable.  I started to draw a series of heart paintings
> (Figure 22).  I came to realize the deepest level of my wound, which hurt me so much.  I was paralyzed.  I
> always tried to run away, and it hurt more.  This time, I sat down by the drawing table surrounded by
> total silence at night.  I stopped resisting what happening to me.*

## 5)  <u>WU WEI 無為</u> : <u>BREAKING THE SHELL</u>

The Chinese believe that the human body is constituted as a micro cosmos; the human
organism is a miniature version of the universe (Maciocia, 1994).  There is a constant struggle in

the human organism, just as in nature, between opposing and unifying forces (Cooper, 1981). According to Tao, wholeness can only be found and cherished by surrendering the mind to the Tao (Morgan, 1974; Cleary, 1991; Richards, 1989). That is the only guarantee, the only sure basis for our wholeness. Here surrender refers to empting oneself or humbling oneself (Maurer, 1985).

Emptiness is linked to the Tao, the Way. The Tao has emptiness as its origins: "The Tao is an empty vessel…" (Tao Te Ching in Wing, 1986, Chapter 4), yet it functions to animate existence only by means of emptiness. Emptiness relates to fullness (Cheng, 1994; Richards, 1989). Indeed, emptiness enables all things that are full to attain their complete fullness. Thus, Lao-tzu could say, "The Tao is an empty vessel; that is its usefulness. But never does it run out or brim over" (Tao Te Ching in Wing, 1986, Chapter 4). Lao-tzu uses concrete examples to demonstrate the usefulness of emptiness:

> Thirty spokes converge at one hub;
> What is not there makes the wheel useful.
> Clay is shaped to form a vessel;
> What is not there makes the vessel useful.
> Doors and windows are cut to form a room.
> What is not there makes the room useful.
> Therefore, take advantage of what is there,
> By making use of what is not.
> (Tao Te Ching in Wing, 1986, Chapter 11)

Through emptiness, the heart can become the model or a mirror for itself and the world; the mind can get away from bias and prejudice. In processing emptiness and being identified with the original emptiness, the Tao, mankind finds itself as a "subject" at the source of images and forms. He/she grasps the rhythm of space and time, and he/she masters the laws of transformation (Cheng, 1994; Wilber, 1999, 2000; Wing, 1986; Richards, 1989).

> What is curved becomes whole;
> What is crooked becomes straight.
> What is deep becomes filled;
> What is exhausted becomes refreshed.
> What is small becomes attainable;
> What is excessive becomes confused.
> Thus Evolved individuals hold to the One
> And regard the world as their pattern.
> (Tao Te Ching in Wing, 1986, Chapter 22)

Pain helps us to grow, to discover the hidden treasures of spiritual wealth we did not know existed within us. Life is a series of painful letting our old-self die, but on the other side is the new life; letting go of the old is embracing the new. The journey of healing is between what you once were and who you are now becoming. We may move one step forward, and slide backs two steps. For sure, we will move in and out of crisis and adversity, and our joys will live alongside of our sorrows (Lord, 1987; Bertman, 1999; Morris, 1971). Tin-en continued to draw her wounded heart.  She explained, "I start to understand what you mean by 'empty your heart.'  I did not know I needed to go through the pain first.  It's painful…."

The Emptiness is also linked to the "Wu. 無"  Wu means nothing or non-being in phenomena but may not mean nothing or non-being in reality (Wing, 1986; Maurer, 1985).   Wu indicates that it is like nothing in the phenomenal world, yet it may be something in reality (Blofeld, 1973).   "Wu-wei" means, "Doing nothing."  Lao-tzu says,  "Through non-action nothing is left undone.  The world is always held without effort.  The moment there is effort, the world is beyond holding" (Tao Te Ching in Wing, 1986, Chapter 48).  This concept is,

> …Not a negative restraint or a holding back from life, but a moving forward and a reaching out to the beyond-words reality of Tao.  Nothing doing is actually a way of getting things done; it is also the only way of doing things with the vigor and persuasiveness that results from following the Way. (Maurer, 1985, p. 21)

Blofeld also (1973) suggests that,
> Wu-wei is not doing by not doing, but acting in a manner that entails the least involvement and proceeds from the inner stillness of the heart… Do what is free from action and disorder will vanish.  Heaven and earth endure because freedom from consciousness of self endows them with everlastingness (pp. 163-164).

## 6) REALIZATION: WHO AM I?

Through conscious learning in conflicts, we have already made considerable progress in our search for realizing about our position in the society.  We, as "subject" human beings have ability to perceive the larger of influences behind specific social phenomena.  This discovery process is a realization toward "Who I am."  Realization in the Chinese character "悟" means the heart reaches complete understanding.  It is derived from the character of "五" for the five senses, symbolizing all things and completion; "口" for mouth and "心" for heart.  The number "five" represents the five senses: five elements, five colors, five tastes, and five systems of the body.  When the heart is in harmony with the five senses it is aware.  This leads to realization (Young, 1997).

Our feelings come from the five senses: eyes to see, ears to hear, mouth to taste, nose to smell, and body to touch.  Feelings tell us what to do, but we need to know about our feelings before we know what to do.  It is the word "feelings" that is the problem.

> I see the first daffodil coming out from the soil
> She wears a yellow white skirt, dancing in the wind
> The blow on my face, it is a gentle touch
> I smell the grassland; it is fresh and sweet
> I lie down on the green grassland

> Imagining I sleep on the cloud, free and happy
> At night, I lie down on my bed, listening to the raindrop fall
> The rhythm beats my heart.  I taste the life in spring

Aren't the feelings included in every sense of our life?  Feelings are the magic words that make us alive, joyous or sorrowful, laugh or cry.  Feelings require that we open our senses to break through our denial.  This lead to deep questions about ourselves and our world, with intense discomfort, possibly despair but possibly joy.  Feelings let us know what we try hard not to see or to hear: that we do not have control over much.  Feeling leads to opening the windows so that the unknown comes in and the winds of change blow through, so that we can see, we can hear, and we can use our sensations.

Tao is unlimited.  Tao does not provide detailed information about the self; modern psychological theories fill in and enrich our understanding of the formation of the self.  Erikson's (1982) "Eight Stages of Human development" correspond to the principle of Yin & Yang.  According to that principle, growing is a lifelong process.  In each stage, we have to face a choice between crisis and change.  By resolving the inner and outer conflict of Erikson's eight stages, we master the strength for growing and develop eight basic virtues (Erikson, 1959, pp. 53-57; 1982, pp. 32-33).

> Through the transformation in each stage, one may attain spiritual wholeness, integrity, and      wisdom – an authentic self, as Tao says (Wing, 1986).  Murray (1959) addresses that,

> Tao produces all things, its Virtue nourishes them, each is formed according to its nature, each is perfected according to its strength (p. 24)…He who acts in accordance with Tao, becomes one with Tao.  He who treads the path of Virtue becomes one with Virtue. (p. 27)

Giving birth to yourself requires that you ask yourself difficult questions: Who am I?  Who are you?  Am I the living person I want to be?  What have I really been doing my whole entire life?  What is happiness?  And what is pain?  What do I need to let go of to be free?  These questions are the contractions in your rebirth process that will push you through to a new, liberated existence.  Asking and answering these questions require great emotional courage.  It means seeing parts of yourself you have been avoiding or denying.  Birth is never easy.  Considering a mother bearing her child for nine months with patient and love, then get birth her newborn child through pains.  When the parents are holding with this new life with tears, the pains turn into joy and celebrate of life.  So, if you are in the process of giving birth to yourself, know that this is a powerful and sacred time of your life.  Surrender to its currents, and if you get a little frightened of the speed at which you're traveling, whatever you do, don't try to turn and go back the other way.  There is nowhere to go but out.  In addition, the best way is to go through it,

To surf into the deep, which is within, we have to go through the darkness, seeking the light until it is found.  We are cautioned that the way will not be easy.  However, embarking on the journey within one's inner conflicts, repressed memories, unmet potentials, and hidden fears that have been stored in the subconscious mind will uncover all that was covered (Ellenberger, 1970). And everything now hidden will be made clear by the higher teaching, the Tao.  This cleansing and healing is done internally.  The method for turning within, knowing oneself, releasing hidden thoughts and feelings, and finding the true center of one's being is called meditation and inner healing (Richards, 1989; Welwood, 2000).


## 7)  TAO AND TRANSFORMATION


Almost everyone wakes up at least once in a lifetime, and almost everyone goes promptly back to sleep again.  However, through the drowse of their days they still faintly remember that time of awakening.  One of my clients writes,

> Night
> Dark night
> My heart sinks
> I am looking for You upon the sky
> Deep        Dark        Sky
> Solitude
>
> You
> Where are You?
> Where is your promise?
> With my sorrow and worries
> Who can I talk to?
>
> Quiet
> Solitude quiets
> Concentrate        Patient        Waiting
> Suddenly
> A twinkle light appeared at the end of the sky
> It is a bright star
> Oh, It's You
> The twinkle light is not bright as the sun
>
> But, You still here

Chinese philosophy uses part-whole contrasts rather than one-many contrasts:  "In order to apprehend the Tao as phenomena it is necessary to differentiate the particular from the whole and yet fully understand the same particular with reference to the whole" (Ames, 1983, p. 34).  Tao, the way things are, is just the sum of all the Taos of the parts. Cleary (1987) claims this as "the science of essence of life" (pp.  14-16).  The state of experiencing one's perfect union and oneness with the divine is the ultimate purpose of

Tao and the outcome of meditation (Simpkins & Simpkins, 1999; Welwood, 2000).

When the outer and inner integration is achieved, we find ourselves well protected in the realm of immortality. Those who have achieved the "mysterious identity" (Clarke 2000, pp. 140-159) find his/her identity between health and earth. Taoism may be called a kind of natural mysticism (Rowely, 1959; Csikszentmihalyi, 1999; Clarke, 2000). Only instead of seeking union with Tao or the Absolute while ignoring this world, the Chinese sought harmony with the universe by communion with Tao. According to Chang (1963) "to understanding the Tao as an inner experience, we have to distinguish between subject and object vanishes. It is an intuitive, immediate awareness rather than a mediated, inferential or intellectual process" (p. 19).

There are many levels of realization, ranging from temporary experiences, such as Welwood's (2000, pp. 195-201) description of the experience of "Sudden Awakening," to what Wilber (1979, 2000, pp. 122-128) describes as "the transcendent Self" at "one nature with Tao or God." We can find our inner selves, the life of our original nature, through spiritual discipline in contemplation. To be enlightened does not mean seeing other things, but simply seeing oneself; to be discerning does not mean hearing other things, but simply hearing oneself; to be penetrating does not mean knowing other things, but simply knowing oneself. Therefore one's own person is that on which the Way depends. If one's own person is realized, then the Way is realized.

When the Way is open, we will find Tao inside us. Then the 'spirit of Shen' (God's spirit) reveals itself through our existence. As Ames says, "Conducting oneself by following one's original nature is called the Way, acquiring one's heavenly endowment is called virtue" (1983, p. 16). The transformation that occurs through turning within to the word that enlightens all mankind is called realization. Welwood (2000) explains the relationship between transformation and realization,

> *Realization is the movement from personality to being – leading toward liberation form the prison of the conditioned self. Transformation involves drawing on this realization to penetrate the densely conditioned patterns of body and mind, so that the spiritual can be fully integrated into the personal and the interpersonal, so that the personal life can become a transparent vessel for ultimate truth or divine revelation (p. 195).*

# II.  PART TWO

## THE INTEGRATION JOURNAL

I have always been interested in the transformation process, especially within the context of art creation.   I began my study with an experience I had with my father, something he taught me.   My earliest childhood memories of art are of watching my father drew.   I cannot forget the shadow of his back as he concentrated on drawing during the middle of many nights. He always told me, " The most important thing in a portrait is the spirit of the person.   You have to observe carefully.   There are different characteristics in every human being."  The portrait has to capture his/her "Spirit of Shen" (神韻).  In Chinese characters, the symbol of "Shen" （神） is interpreted as "God": "Shen indicates thinking, consciousness, insight and memory, and all five mental-spiritual aspects of being human, all of which depend on the heart." (Maciocia, 1994, p. 200).

At that time, I was too young to understand what my father was saying.   But when I looked at his drawings (figure 1, 2 ), there was a magnetic attraction that drew me to search for "Shen"-- the inner spirit of people.   This attraction is not because his paintings were famous; the drawings are a bridge between us.  My father tried to send a message through drawing, and I tried to understand it.

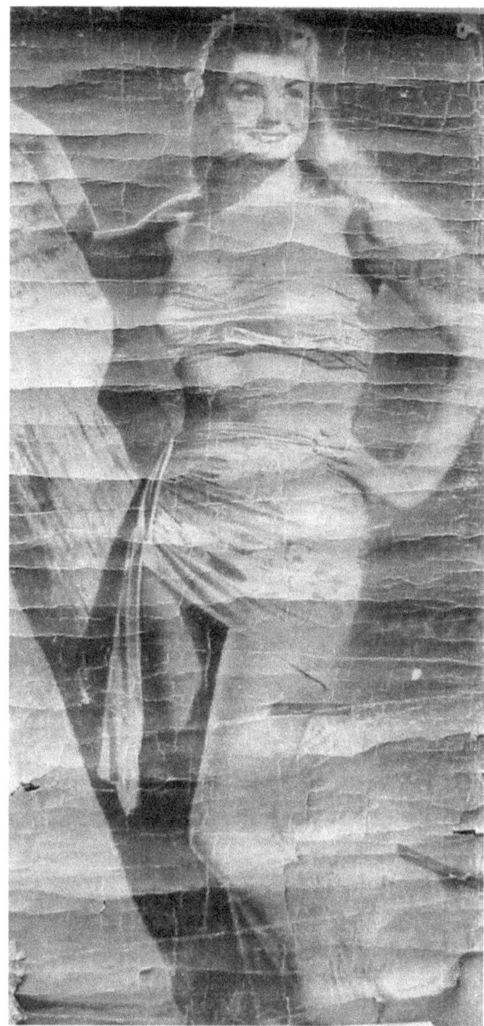

Figure 1.  Ester Williams      Charcoal Painting

Figure 2.  Mr. Yu              Oil Painting

## 1)   ART AS A RELATIONSHIP WITH THE SELF

I am always amazed by watching clients' facial expression and gesture after they finished a drawing. It announces to the world: "I, the artist, was here, and I had something to say. Here it is! Yes, This is I!" Drawings, paintings, sculptures, symphonies, poems, dances, and dramas are not simply ideas. Each brushstroke, each chiseled hollow; every harmony, every internal rhyme; all dance steps, are snapshots of life, pieces of reality (Goleman, Kaufman, Ray, 1992; Bateson, 1989; Jensen, 1997).

When my father's artwork is in front of me, I try first to listen from my heart. There is a subtle silence. I hear the sound of his brush caressing oil paints on the canvas. As the sounds grow louder and vividly, I catch a mumbled word or two, perhaps a scream or a sigh, maybe a laugh. Though I try to sense my father's mood, the expression of emotion and thoughts through art is seldom projected upon any audience first. On the contrary, the artist talks to the self from inside first. It is an expression from the self to the self (Durfee, 1989; MacPhail, 1974). Many times, my clients explain their feelings to me before I ask them questions. Since nothing can be understood until it has been expressed, clients are not conscious or often as surprised by the nature of the feelings as is his/her audience (Richardson & Rogers, 1998; Swanson, 1999; Betensky, 1973).

As the artist draws the first line on the empty paper, "the image begins its journey from inside to outside" (Personal interview with artist Aaron). As the artist adds lines and shapes, the image grows and defines itself. There is a constant ebb and flow of forces between the artist and the emerging image: emotion, imagination, thinking, and conflicts all have a role (Keyes, 1983). The creative process – "Paving the Way, Incubation, Perchance to Daydreaming, Illumination" – is often deeply moving, filled with unspeakable description (Goleman, Kaufman, Ray, 1992, pp. 18-24; Armstrong, 1986). Only the creator can fully experience the depth of the happenings in his/her heart (MacPhail, 1974).

Art as the relationship with the self is a subjective reaction to the environment that makes art as self-expression. Within each work of art, an artist portrays his/her feelings, and his/her intellectual abilities. Physical development, perceptual sensitivities, emotional expression, creative involvement, social development, and aesthetic awareness are also expressed (Lowenfeld, 1968; Ohler, 2000).

## 2)   ART AS COMMUNICATION WITH OTHERS

If art creates a relationship with the self, art creation is an act of self-expression. If we define art as self-expression, then we have to ask what it is about the self that needs to be expressed. Self-psychology (Young-Eisendrath, 1987) uses many terms to explain the "Self." There is a popular assumption that language, whether oral or written, is so beset with rules and conventions that its use is frequently inhibiting rather than liberating (Igoa, 1999). However, the practice of the visual arts is not influenced by rules, and consequently the individual experiences a sense of freedom when painting that he/she does not experience when writing an essay. This suggests that the need of the self for freedom from the constraints of civilized life finds its fulfillment in the act of artistic creation (Rubin, 1984).

Our daily life experiences contribute to a building-up of frustrations, an accumulation of pent-up energies. In order to live harmoniously with each other, we repress our instinctual desires, and that repression leads to tension. Artistic activity, then, constitutes a socially acceptable and personally rewarding outlet for those energies or tensions. At the same time that the individual solves his/her problem through art, he/she also creates something that is objectively satisfying and aesthetically valuable (Dantus, 1999; Snyder, 1997; Jensen, 1997).

If art is a form of self-expression, it does not occur in a social vacuum. Expression is directed outward, towards someone. That someone affects not only the visible form of artistic expression but also the self that desires communion with another. The most importantly of all, the self is changed in the process of expression by the requirements of the other with whom it desires to communicate. Self-expression then is completed in the form of communication with others (MacPhail, 1974).


## 3)  ART AS SPIRITUAL JOURNEY WITH TAO


It has been said that, "By the single daring assumption of the cosmic principle of the Tao, the Chinese focused on the notion of one power permeating the whole universe" (Rowley, 1955, p. 5). The Tao Te Ching says,

> Something mysteriously formed,
> Born before heaven and earth.
> In the silence of the void,
> Tao is standing alone and unchanging,
> Ever present and in motion.
> Perhaps is the mother of ten thousand things.
> Its true name I do not know.
> Tao is the by-name that we give it.
> (Tao Te Ching in Wing, 1986, Chapter 25)

Tao's concept of "One" makes Chinese artists search for balance and harmony with the universe by communion with Tao. The union with Tao is the ultimate artistic achievement (Rowley, 1955). In my experience of making art, I never know what I am going to paint until I am almost finished with the work. Even when I discipline myself to paint or draw from nature or some life theme, I still, in the deepest sense, do not know why I have chosen a particular subject or how my inner self will direct the execution of the work. The clarification of emotions and thoughts will emerge as the process takes place. I prefer not to think too much while drawing, allowing nature to reveal lines, shapes, and forms in its own way.  It grows out of the wanderings of my heart: heart leads, brush follows.  I have some images in my mind while I paint, but I seldom sketch before I paint, because I want to leave space for the accidental surprise.  Let the strokes take shape themselves.  From here the artist, the object, and the work have a mutual communication and relationship.  My paintings are based on the drawing process in Chinese painting.  I observe things or persons, not only the surfaces, but the inner spirit – chi – that resembles Kandinsky's (1982) idea of "inner sound."  With these experiences, I discover that there is a wheel in my heart generating the creative process.  This wheel includes,

A) Deep observation: I observe with my spirit and soul.  In some moment, I may lose myself in it.

B) Rational individualization: I know something is not equivalent to how I understand it.  I understand some things are not necessary to my life.  When I am watching a clock, it is not merely a time or a date.  The importance emerges from where I put myself in it.  Listening to the "Tei Tec" sound, I also hear my heart beat.  It pushes me to understand in a deeper sense that my life is running away with these long and short needles.  I can even see life and death through this clock.  Then I can understand that death is not only the time when you go back to the dust.  When I was born, death became connected to my life between time and space.

C) Strong affection: is rooted from my deep observation and rational individualization.  Only I have this strong affection, only I can put it into my artwork.  Strong affection is my potential for creation.

D) Transformation: is a compressor for the creative process.  It enables my strong feelings to transform into an ideal world.  I can imagine the gestures of dancers, as flying swans, trees in the forest … it are the power of transformation.

E) Sublimation: I can unite my feelings of reality with the everlasting, infinite Being (Tao) through a constant transformation process.  I can obtain my existence.  With this wheel of creation, I enter the journey of my inner self, others, and the universe.


## 4)  ART PSYCHOTHERAPY


Art therapy bridges our inside and outside worlds, our fantasy and our reality.  Here, the most important issue is our "honesty."  From honesty, springs forth love, so that we can heal. Art has a role  to  nurture  our  soul  and  characters,  but  also healing  power (Naumbury, Kramer, 1955). Art is a direct expression of human inner world.  In  the  therapeutic process, like a midwife, therapist witness the birth of the inner self from my clients' deepest and hidden places.   It is a process, which involves pains, love, fears, tears, angers, ignorance, brokenness,  humor,  laughter  and  wisdom….  As a result, artistic creation process became psychological treatment.

According to the America Art Therapy Association, the International Expressive Art Therapy

Network: Art (music, art, drama and etc.) are powerful tools for psychological assessment and healing. It is like an open-heart surgery: arts bridge our inner and outer being, connect to our subconscious mind (spiritual, intellectual, and emotional and behavior being). It also: -

- *can provide a non-threatening avenue to involve clients in the therapeutic process.*
- *can loosen rigidity and encourage age-appropriate risk taking.*
- *can allow for the ventilation and the working through of overwhelming feelings.*
- *can help unlock experiences and facilitate the healing of painful issues.*
- *can circumvent verbal manipulation and get to the source of the problem quicker.*
- *can confront and reduce denial by providing a tangible record of feelings and thoughts.*
- *can help with problem solving, decision-making and improving judgment making skills.*

The clinician needs to observe as closely as possible the manner in which each individual precedes and how he/she works. While listening to music or drawing a picture, client may re-experience the traumatic past. A trained professional knows why, what, how, when to direct or not to execute the process. And the most important part is to support the flash-black moments, and heal the wound.

| Art Therapy Is | Is Not |
|---|---|
| 1. Psychoanalytic | Fortune Teller |
| 2. Assessment & Treatment | Drawing |
| 3. Understand | Labels |
| 4. Process | Product |
| 5. Discover Creativity | Artistic Talents |
| 6. Problem Solving | Medicine |
| 7. Dealing with Emotion | Magic |

The art therapist cannot eliminate the pains, but we can turn the suffering into blessings. The therapeutic process, like most creative processes, is messy, confusing and even ugly. Only with an aesthetic sense, can one see beauty in ugliness. Only with a heart of compassion, can one touches human dignity and integrity. Only with a mind of hope and trust can one turns fantasy into reality? Only with an empty spirit, can one creates something from nothing and embraces paradox.

## 5)  <u>PHENOMENOLOGICAL INVESTIGATION OF HEALING IN ART</u>

I assimilate Stanage's (1987) phenomenological approach of "Feelings, experiencing and consciousing" into the investigation of healing in art.

Feb 7, 1995

I picked up pink chalk and started to draw.  I placed the chalk horizontally on the paper, so that I could draw a wider area.  I drew a curved line.  I asked myself what it was.

*Thoughts come across my head… I hardly feel able to get close to my inner feelings.  Something is blocking my feelings.*

I picked up black chalk and drew a flat line on the pink line.  It formed an eye shape close to the end of the paper.

*The black line draws my attention to my schooling.  I am frustrated about my study.  Things I need to learn do not seem grounded in my life.  Something is missing.  Perhaps it is my culture, maybe my feeling. I do not know how to express myself.  Sometimes I have refused to learn.*

I picked up yellow chalk and filled in the eyes.

*I need something bright and cheerful.*

Then, I added some red and green around the eye.  I filled in the space with orange and purple.  The shape was expanded.  I added some shadow with light blue and yellow.  An abstract form was shifted.  It looked like a deformed human figure.

*As the shape expands, I think it is my "shifting." I recognize that I have learned to be flexible in a new country.  I need to adapt to the system, even though sometimes I do not like it.  As time goes by, I am deformed as the picture.*

The telephone rang; my sister who lives in Canada was on the phone.  While I was listening to her, I picked up a pencil and continued my drawing.  I added shadows and darkened the margins.  The shape stood up clearly.

*I ignore my inner feelings.  I am almost paralyzed.*

The deformed figure (Figure 3) was completed, but it was changing.

*Perhaps I am changing.  Life is a dynamic change within my two cultures and background.*

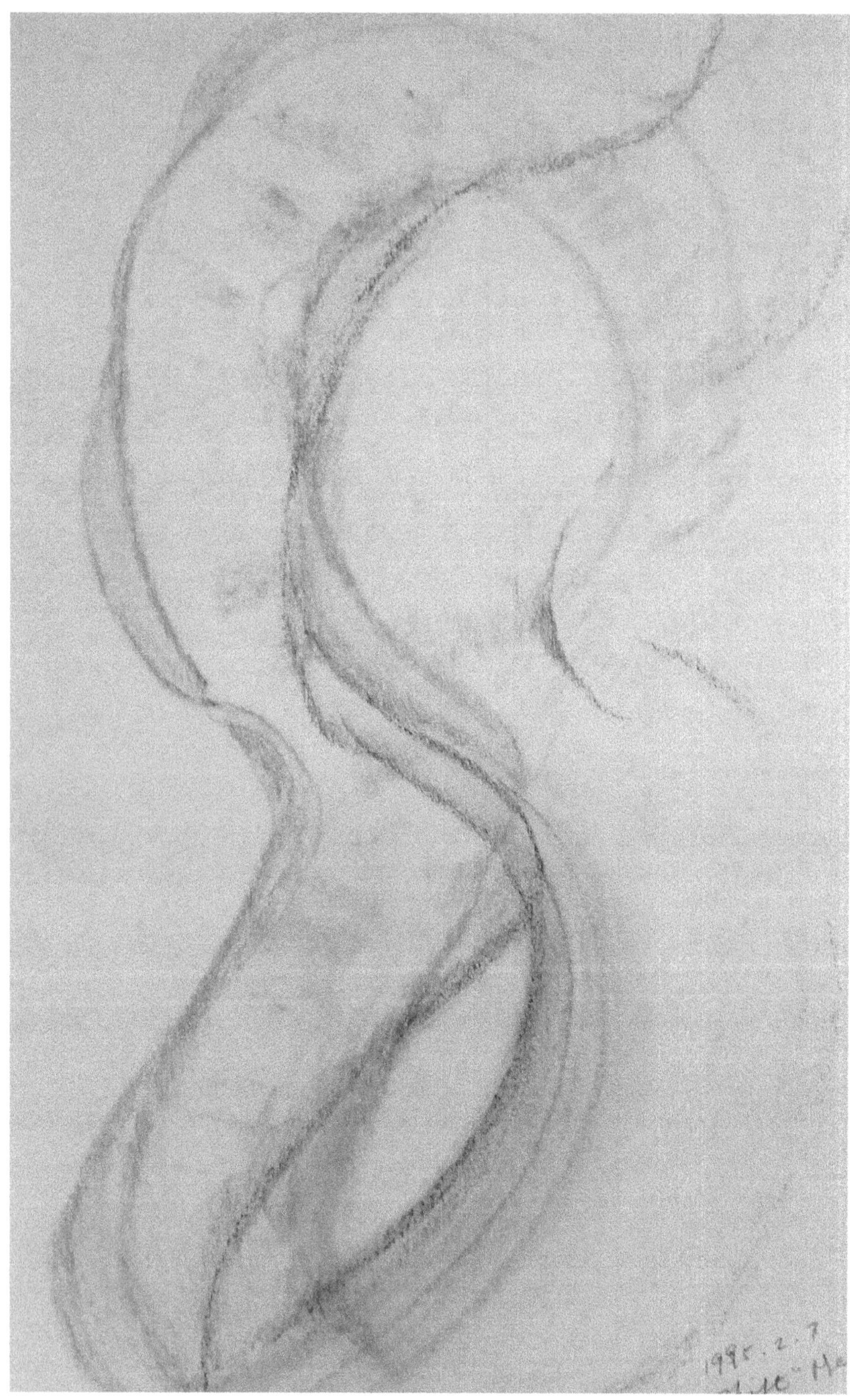

Figure 3.  Deformed Figure          Pastel

## How the Experience Occurred

I experience of making the art object occurred through the volition/intention of myself, the physical activities of making, the process of expanding the field of meaning through analogues and by forming meaning.

1. Through my own volition
   I attempted to contact and express my inner experience: visual images, expectations, conceptions, meanings and feelings. This implicit experience was the stuff of the making, the ground of experience that the materials and activities helped to make more explicit.

2. Through the physical activities
   I involve in making the art object -- mixing the paint, moving  the brush through space and space, forming the clay, stopping, sitting and looking-- I engaged with external objects and attempted to bring forth my inner experience.

3. Through the relax and free atmosphere,
   I gradually experienced a transition in my experience of making. I let go " of conscious concerns" for accurate representation on my inner visual image; pervious knowledge of the formal qualities of art; expectations about having a show, using canvas, and good paint; and other conceptions, idea and concerns for what other people might think of me and my painting.

4. I became more open and accepting of what I was involved with in the experience of making the art object. "By accepting the materials, letting go of expectations and realizing I had to forget about everything…" Rather than trying to place my expectation on the objects of the art making, a seemingly one-way process that blocked the flow of my experiencing, there was an interactive or dialogue sense of movement and energy a flowing in as well as a flowing out.

5. The meaning emerged in a manner that was:
   1) Dialectic.  For example, *"I picked up a yellow chalk, filled in the eyes" "I need something bright and cheerful."*
   2) Interactive.  For example, *"As the shape is expanding, I think it is my shifting perspective.  I recognize I have learned to be flexible in a new country.  I need to adapt to the system, even though sometimes I do not like it.  As time goes by, I am deformed as the picture."*
   3) Synergistic.  For example, *"Perhaps I am changing.  Life is a dynamic change within my two cultures"* (Valle & King, 1978).

The following paintings were done 25 years ago. It illustrated the process of my transformation through art.

<u>List of Drawings (figure 4~15)</u>

4)  The Self  (Cover)     30"x60" Ink & water color on rice paper
5)  Conflicts     28"x28" Ink & water color on rice paper
6)  Trapped     28"x28" Ink & water color on rice paper
7)  Break     28"x28" Ink & water color on rice paper
8)  Where to go?     30"x60" Ink & water color on rice paper
9)  Mask     28"x28" Ink & water color on rice paper
10)  Hanging there     28"x28" Ink & water color on rice paper
11)  Steps     30"x60" Ink & water color on rice paper
12)  Dynamic flux     28"x28" Ink & water color on rice paper
13)  Alive     28"x28" Ink & water color on rice paper
14)  Breaking through     28"x32" Ink & water color on rice paper
15)  Soring free     30"x60" Ink & water color on rice paper

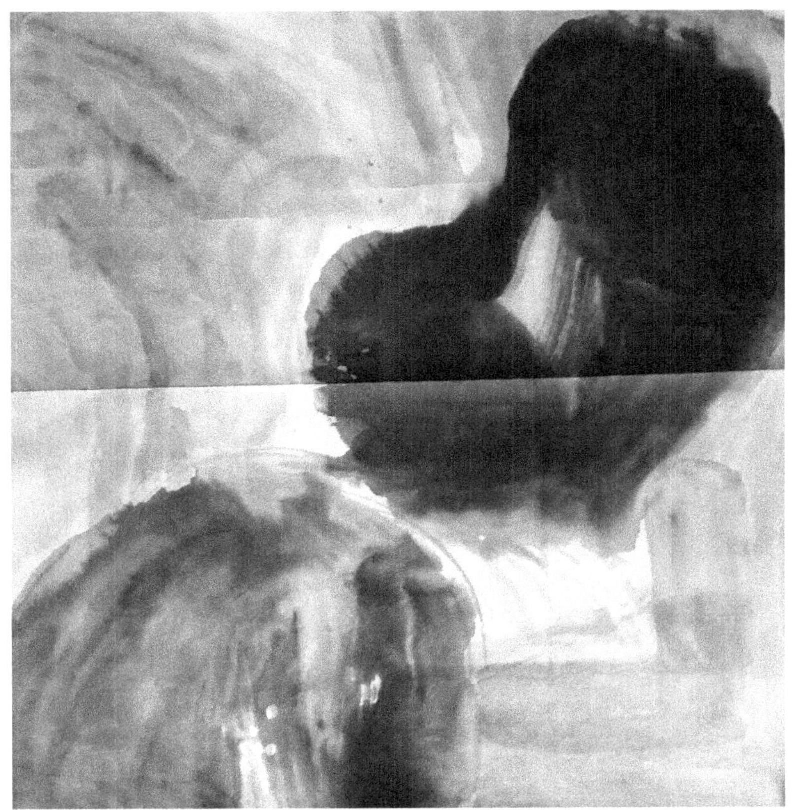

Figure 5      Conflict  矛盾

Figure 6    Trapped    困

Figure 7     Break          折

Figure 8       Where to go?          何去何從

Figure 9      Mask      面具

Figure 10      Hanging There      縣空

Figure 11        Steps        踪跡

Figure 12        Dynamic Flux        動態聯盟

Figure 13     Alive     生

Figure 14     Breakthrough     突破

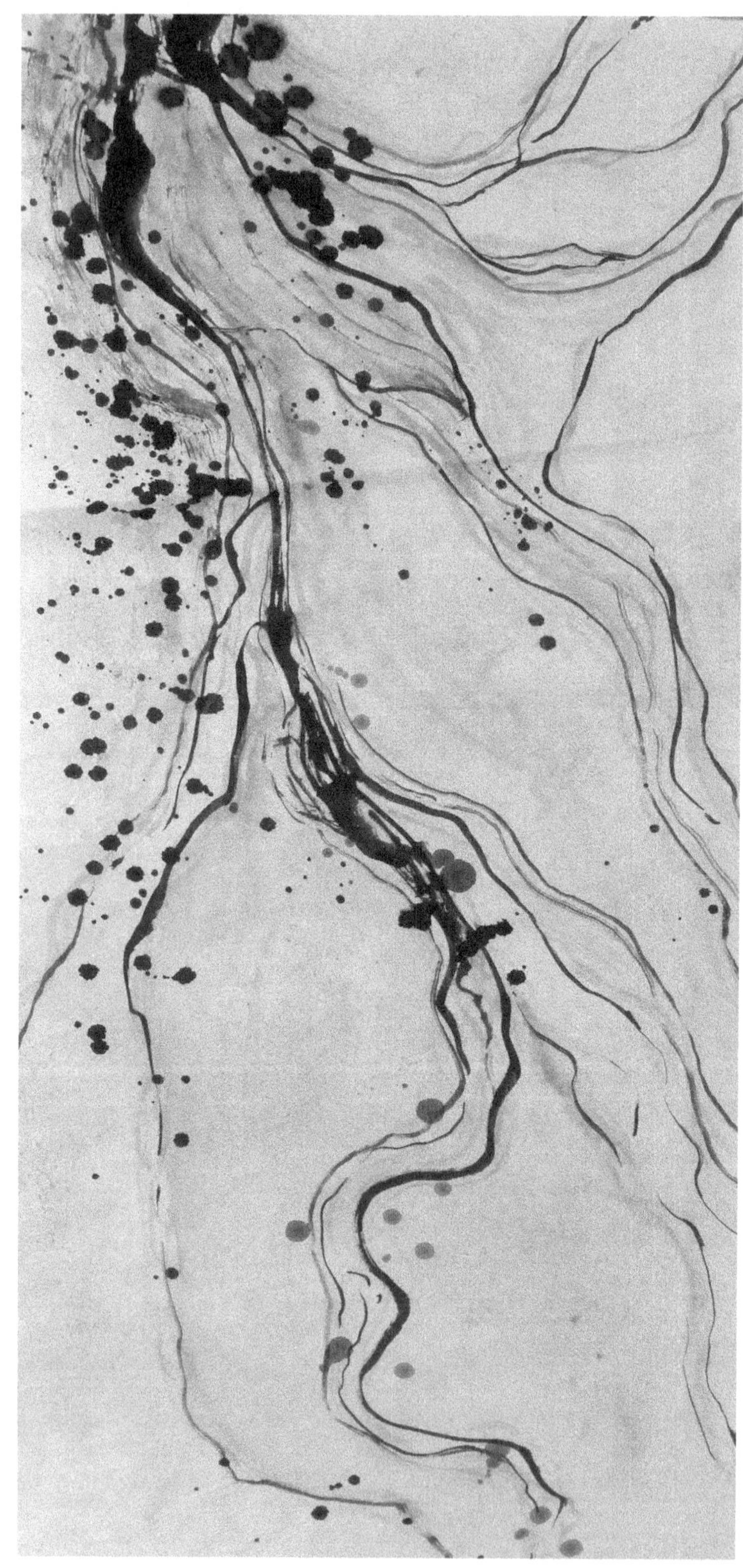

Figure 15      Soar Free      翔空

## 6   ART PSYCHOTHERAPY AND CHINESE ART

The following conversation was recorded when talking about art psychotherapy and Chinese Art with Master John Chen.  Master Chen is a well-known Chinese ink artist and resides in Vancouver.

August 2017

Lau: From children art teacher to art therapist, books you sent to me have changed my career life. It is nice to be able to discuss psychology and art with you today. You are the founder of the "Association of Heartfelt traditional Chinese Painting",  Can you talk about what is the origin?

Chen: Heartfelt imagery is the source of my creativity, because the heart is the motive force of flexible thinking and it controls feelings. Heartfelt imagery is a transformation of spirit which has a transforming and circulating function that can produce innumerable kinds of behavior with aggregating or dispersing the separation and combining of thoughts. Heartfelt imagery synthesizes rationality and perception. It unites together the beauty of Nature and the eternity of inner life. It can expand the space of imagination, constantly exchanging intellectuality with passion and promoting the development of art.

Lau: It is wonderful that summarize a person's rationality, sensibility, behavior and spiritual state. Rather than a lot of modern fragmentation of philosophical thinking, or just a single theory of emphasis. Recently, your exhibition -- displaying part of 252 meters long "The love for Rocky Canada" Chinese landscape painting in the city of Richmond City Hall, where did the motive come from?

Chen: Since moved from Taiwan to Canada 26 years ago, I was moved by the natural landscape of North America, and deeply fell in love with this land. Every year driving to the Rocky Mountains and sketch the beautiful scenery. In order to create the landscape, it has been in mind for 26 years and spent a full six years to do that. I started painting from the UBC Anthropological Museum and then traveled through Stanley Park, Capilano Suspension Bridge, the town of Hope, along the Rocky Mountains eastbound to Banff National Park, to Jasper National Park.  Drawing the four seasons, round a circle, until the return to my home near UBC.  Over the years accumulated hundreds of paintings, selected from 142 connected to the total length of 252 meters long landscape. From the painting, you can see the Rock Canyon forest canyon, symbol of Aboriginal culture totem rock paint columns, scenic alpine lakes and thousands of waterfall glaciers.

Lau: I heard that there are some inner stories lead to this creative motives, what is it?

Chen: When I was young, I asked my parents: Where did I come from? They said that I came from the edge of the water, the stone burst back. So I love nature. Ha Ha

Lau: Here art brings a positive energy to you. But this answer: similar to your story, in clients

I met may cause a negative and unhealthy emotions. Can you explain how art giving you the power of positive spirit?

Chen: The heart can leap over all material and spiritual obstacles. It is said: My heart is the universe and the universe is my heart. My heart can make a spiritual tour of the universe with no limits; it is free, optimistic and progressive… Therefore, value heartfelt imagery and embrace true feelings is the central core of creativity. And reach the Zen domain of "all realms are revealed in the heart".
The goals of the heart are limitless and can include everything. In concrete images and abstractions: there are ideals, fantasies, dreams, meditations, wishful thinking, reflections, mental associations, imagination and recollection. All these are the origins of artistic creativity.

Lau: Here I understand the heartfelt, as "Depth Psychology" "Ego Self" ". Self is not equal to the Chinese people interprets as "selfish". Self- contains inner and external psychological growth, the so-called knowing ourselves and the need. Different age stages have different psychological virtues of the training exercise. You just mentioned a lot of different ideas and thinking. There may be crooked, unrealistic, not constructive thoughts. How to distinguish it? From an artistic point of view, all seems to be an acceptable ideas. In painting market, such as Van Gogh's paintings in his life time nobody cherished; after death was used as market value. In the art therapist's point of view, each painting is very precious, it is a bridge of communication between people.

Chen: There are two directions for heart's intent: one inward, one outward. Therefore, "heart's direction" determines the artist's painting methods and views, and carefully opens up new territory according to one's own interests and theories. The one is directed inward, and can explore "true images"; the other is directed outward, and can gain more outside "false images". These images are causing creativity to stay between "being and non-being", similar and dissimilar, with countless changes. Therefore, an artist needs to have both orientations, let "heartfelt imagery" live both inside and outside the gate of orientations. One must not just work behind closed doors or roam widely with no purpose.

Lau: In research of the creation process, it is the realm of learning the integration of: the left and right brain functions, sensation and rational, reality and fantasy, conscious and subconscious. It seems that if you cannot distinguish between "true images" and "false images", there is no "heartfelt" images?

Chen: In tradition, the true image 真象 is spiritual discussion. In order to produce good artwork, artists should be able to handle the real life. The truth of art is the essence of the Tao. Creative artists express the true image form his/her inner spirit, more than the outward false image 假象 material illusion description. Although in the development of modern art, there are changing images 變象; the existence and development of the heartfelt is no change. In the realm of performance, constant change is existed, but, its' essence are similar since ancient times.

Lau:     Can I say: The truth image 真象 is the image of the spirit, the cultivation of the mind. The false image 假象 is the image of the object, the outward material description.  And the heartfelt image  心象 is the unity of mind and body integration within Tao.  Tao can transcend all the limitations of our bodies, thoughts, emotions, and social systems. In many different schools of art history, works can show the heartfelt image.  It depends on the artist's spiritual cultivation?

Chen:    The true image is mostly scientific dialectical reality. The false image is the illusion of the subjective misjudgment of the impression. The true image is true.  The false image is often the illusion of the beauty which resulting in a different phenomenon. The true image is a natural phenomenon.  The false image is the phenomenon illusion of individual factors.  In Chinese art history, the unity between heaven and self with Tao is the ultimate achievement. The fusion between material and self in the doctrine of mean.

Lau:     So abstract painting, surrealist are true image or not? The fusion between material and self is the heartfelt image?

Chen:    Abstract is not necessary the entire true image. The abstract is the concrete side, but often mistakenly abstract, but it is true image.  The real situation has, for example, the amplification of flower, rock mechanism. It was misunderstood as abstract painting, because it is not common.  The so-called reality tangible and intangible distinction, invisible as the spirit, thought. Surrealism has the meaning of reproduction of things, also close to the truth of the natural thing.  The fusion between material and self is the first heartfelt image of the heart; is the root of the creation into new image. "Image comes from the heart" That is: heart is the cause; the fruit is from the causal relationship.

Lau:      It answers my question that I have been struggling to understand the nature of true and false in human problems.  As the artist sees, the scientist may not see it at all.  Although the scientific research enhance the modern civilization, it is dialectical to one-sided, to slice the whole or to go extreme and become fragmented. Does not contain a comprehensive and the depth of the heart. There will no way to talk about fusion and union between the spirit and the self.

Chen:    In principle, the true image will not change or a few change.  The false image is unstable, will change from different people, time and place.

Lau:     Because in essence, truth and goodness is eternal. And the theory of relativity can be mixed!

Chen:    Fusion between spirit and heart should be like a pictographic, project feelings in the material. Relativity theory in the artistic creation, there is a reverse reflection. It may be good.

Lau: You mean in the performance of the painting layout, a painting has a framework, which is like an    analogy of absolute. Within the range of framework, relative theory is good. In psychology, within the principle of truth and goodness in human nature, using relative theory to gain insight of self-understanding and interpersonal relationship.  Artistic thinking is wide and deep! Even crazy ideas can be! Then in the modern trend – Intentional Expressionism, how can artists reveal heartfelt image through hidden preconscious and subconscious?

Chen: With the movement of will, it can be intentionally expressed.  But the essence heart 本心

, the original heart 初心 is not yet emerging. Intention to pursue, but slowly will find demons. The original heart of the human is in the human spirit, after positive and negative reflection, the artist must be a wise sword, focusing on spiritual cultivation. The mind is not blindfolded in order to be able to understand, and constantly explore the pursuit of the truth of life and beauty. The truth is primitive.  Goodness can be nurture through the social culture, education induced moral rope.

Lau: So, you are saying that a work of art can emerge the original and essence of heartfelt is an art of life – it is alive.  If there is no intention of the heart, then the artistic creation of no sense of life. This argument is like in the process of art therapy treatment, the therapist encourage clients to paint through subconscious mind, to explore and induce the direction. In this way, even the works are ugly, finished or not finished; are the art of life!

Chen:  I added: 1. Inward experience and outward observation, that is, outside the fortune, through our inner heart. On the Unification of the Two Systems of Cosmic Ontology. The deeper the outward perception, the stronger the inward insight. It is also the integration of human and nature into one, the unity of human and heaven. 2. Advanced cognition is more than the artistic level, to pursue a higher philosophical meaning, in the field of limited art development to the infinite space, so the Chinese painting art to conform to the times, but also beyond the times. 3. In the present and the performance of unity, rationality in the irrational integration, the expression of the artist's spiritual nature, does not violate the human nature. 4. Closed together, the four inclusive of the painting together, do not do extreme opposition or waste.

Lau: Master's art work highlights the sublimation of life to the noble nature of the natural landscape: "Heaven and Man" follow with the heart. I have been tasted a moment insight of this experience once, but soon returned to reality. Up the mountain still have to go down to the valley, I chose the art therapy to reveal the truth and kindness through the therapeutic creative process.  Teacher's encouragement to inspire me to remember my original heart: life from fantasy to the real world. Art bridges our inside and outside worlds, our fantasy and our reality.  Here, the most important issue is our "honesty."

From honesty, springs forth love, so that we can heal.  The therapeutic process, like most creative processes, is messy, confusing and even ugly.  Only with an aesthetic sense can one see beauty in ugliness.  Only with a heart of compassion can one touch human dignity and integrity.  Only with a mind of hope and trust can one turn fantasy into reality.  Only with an empty spirit, can one create something from nothing and embrace paradox.

Chen:    Yes, look at the world with the beauty heart!  Do not care good or bad, beauty ugly ... ... the heart is the source of  artistic creation.  Heartfelt Art is the expression of the artist's inner spiritual world, the interpretation of truth and kindness.  The spiritual content of human thought can carry forward to the world, and made the difference.

Lau:    These paintings I did when I was writing dissertation.  Art is inconceivable. 25 years ago, I did not know what I painted. Now realize a deeper understanding and have meanings in me (figure 4~ 15).

Chen:    Life journey is like ECG, is beating.  If no beating, life will end. The process of artistic creation, if not contain before and after, it is the endless artistic life. Thoughts in 25 years ago is existence of subconscious.  That is the fact that my so-called artistic life contains past, present, future. This is what I often mentioned to my graduate students.

Lau:    Can you interpret the past, now, the future theory more?

Chen:    The past, present, the future, the mutation of the true image probability is not too much. The two poles, the doctrine of the mean will not disappear. This is the   reason that the heartfelt image can determine the cause of our work, but also the true image is greater than the false image.

Lau:    Ah! No wonder many clients thought I could predict their life! In fact, we have the skills of intuitive and insight into the heart! I think there is a lot of connection between your idea of art and psychotherapy.

Chen:    The development trend of modern art, mostly from perception to intuition, from the objective to the subjective, from the concrete to the abstract, from rational to emotional, in fact, are all emphasized to express their feelings, thoughts and intuitive feelings, this is the confession of heart. Everything to pursue from the root, we have loyal to our own heart.  With objective philosophy to verify, cherish the existence of individual, make good use of harmonious relativism and absolute coexistence

Lau:    Yes, never forget the original heart! This is what I wrote more than a decade ago: "Tao, Art and Mental Health".  Modern philosophical thinking only take the relative and to abandon the absolute, resulting in a lot of soul empty. I am very satisfied for what I did in my office silently. And now have time to create artwork again.  I need to dialogue with your heartfelt art theory.  It should be able to broaden the field of art.  I just want people to understand the truth, kindness and the beauty in art – ultimate human treasures.

Chen:   The enthusiasm for art is the first condition for artistic creation. When the painting is cultivated, it is meaningful to have a good life.  Art nurture our soul and life. On the basis of the existing find a way out to play, no pressure. Find the future, the joy of the heart, abundant in life.

Lau:   Thank you Master Chen, your time and guidance! And spent time for the Chinese proofreading and summary for this book.  Congratuation for your painting "The love for Rocky Canada" create the world's longest Chinese landscape painting in the process. There are still a lot of things to do. Wishing you a healthy body, mind, heart and spirit to finish it, and to flourish the Chinese art spiritual civilization in the Western culture!

# III.   PART THREE

## THE LIFE LONG LEARNING JOURNAL

The Tao is limitless. It provides us unlimited opportunities to learn and grow. The experience of Tao is analogous to the creativity of the artist.  The Tao of living cultivates the unity of life in its dynamic flux.  The view of Tao draws attention to the psychological, aesthetic, and spiritual realm, often-neglected dimensions of life and adult Education.  The Tao of living, which is an orientation towards the source and unity of life and being, transcends the petty problems of the mundane world and the institutions of society.  This is a lifelong learning task. The Tao of lifelong learning is focused on developing success, "emptying oneself" of biases, egocentrism, degradation, and ethnocentrism or on cultivating a sense of "consciousness" through self-corrective participation and reflection.

## 1) THE MEANING OF SELF

We may experience times of extremity: a great deal of ugliness or beauty, a great deal of hurt or love, a great deal of loneliness or intimacy. At these moments, we begin to look beyond, to feel in our marrow and possible to cry out that, "this can't be all." We may begin to search for a life fulfilled by wider and deeper meanings, split off into many different religions or spiritual directions. Jesus speaks of our Father in heaven; the Buddha describes the nature within you and also within all creatures; Confucian cries out for Heaven; the philosophers speak of humans as a microcosm mirroring the macrocosm in all respects. Whether the message is in an image or a word, it conveys meanings in life.

I believe every psychological struggle is a search for spiritual direction. I also share with Young-Eisendrath (2000), a belief that "psychotherapy is a relationship founded on human suffering, attempting to alleviate it through an awakening" (p. 136). Because of the nature of suffering, spiritual questions like "Why are we here?", "Who am I?", "What about pains and happiness?", or "Where are we going?" are easily raised during a session. I respond with respect and curiosity. Young-Eisendrath points out, it is a conviction that suffering wills someday make sense and that life has a purpose that goes beyond one's own identity. Sometimes, maybe often, it is the patient's first authentic and sustained experience of the 'unspeakable' unity of existence – the unnamable that is called God, the Tao, True Nature, and the like (p. 139).

According to Jung's (1971), thinking and feeling are opposites on the rational axis. When the two poles of this axis are brought together, as when an upsetting feeling is appropriately named, a small miracle occurs in psychotherapy: a union of opposites in which a whole is sensed (Clarke, 1994; Watts, 1961). It is important to bring psychological opposites into conscious awareness for the sake of psychic health and vitality. Jung (1965) bridges the wisdom of the Tao and psychotherapy: we see a light to achieve a balanced way of living between heaven and earth. He says,

> If we take Tao as the method or conscious way by which to unite what is separated, we have probably come quite close to the psychological content of the concept…Without doubt also, the question of making opposites conscious means reunion with the laws of life represented in the unconscious, and the purpose of this reunion is the attainment of conscious life, or, expressed in Chinese terms, the bringing about of Tao. (pp. 95-96)

The value of Tao lies in its power to reconcile opposites on a higher level of consciousness. It is symbolically expressed as light in Taoism. "To reconcile the polarities, is to achieve a balanced way of living and a higher integration" (Change, 1963, p. 5). The absolute and relative values are not contradictory: "…a thing is the focus of relationships determined by its context in the whole" (Ames, 1983, p. 35). To reconcile the polarities in order to achieve a balanced way of living and a higher integration is the endeavor of psychotherapy. Jung (1965) found out that the method he had applied for years in his practice coincided with the wise teaching of the ancient Tao. He says,

My experience in my practice has been such as to reveal to me a quite new and unexpected approach to Eastern wisdom… my professional experiences have shown me that in my technique I had been unconsciously led along the secret way which for centuries has been the preoccupation of the best minds of the East. (In Chang, 1963, p. 6)

Beyond our limitations, there are still a lot of opportunities to learn and grow. Between Heaven and Earth, the inside and outside world, mind and heart, rational and emotional, holding or let go, there are endless ways to learn. Our strength is usually also our weakness. With fragmentation and specialization in the modern society, overdeveloped virtues or strengths will also indicate those underdeveloped virtues and weaknesses. Welwood (1991) says that, "Becoming human means discovering our fullness and learning to live from it. This involves bringing forth more of who we really are and becoming more available to whatever life presents" (p. 15).

We often find ourselves in the middle of a dilemma: What should I do about the fact that somebody is angry with me? What should I do about the fact that I am angry with somebody? Basically, we do not place our judgment. We are trying to learn not to split ourselves between good and bad, between our pure side and our impure side. We do not try to solve the problem, but instead to use it as a question about how to let this every situation wake up further. We can use different situation to heal ourselves, to encourage ourselves to take a leap, to step out into that ambiguity. Thus, we can say, "I don't know where I am going, but I am on the Way." There are two ways, free or not free, this is our choice in every moment. Life is only a learning process. We can let it remind us that the teachings encourage precision and gentleness, with loving and kindness toward every moment. Our spirituality is not confined to one particular area; otherwise, it would easily create distortion. Spiritual practiced and personal growth is an integral and natural part of living.

Mastery of self is a lifelong journey requiring integrative learning through childhood to old age. Tao is a lifelong learning experience achieved by daily effort. Grigg (1999) says, "No magic, nothing extraordinary is involved. Skills are earned by reflection, by insight, and by cultivated intuitions" (p. 151). Tao is a holistic experience, an interwoven pattern of action-inaction (Yin and Yang) and multiplicity-unity (divergence-convergence) (Chang, 1963, pp. 19-54). Freedom emerges within "Concientizationperson"; not from the dictates of government or social institutions, which mandate "equality" studies and policies. The learner must develop an attitude for success: "emptying oneself" of biases, egocentrism, degradation, class, and ethnocentrism in order to fill up with new potential and knowledge. He/she needs to develop a sense of "consciousness" through self-reflection, correction, and participation.

## 2) <u>TAO, ART AND LIFELONG LEARNING</u>

Tao is a phenomenon that can only be achieved by experiencing a balanced way of living and a higher integration of consciousness (Wilber, 1999; Clarke, 2000). Grigg (1999) says, "The business of human consciousness is meaning…all experience is a disjointed tangle that must be organized and integrated into meaningful patterns by each thinking person" (p. 146). The tenth chapter of the Tao Te Ching, "Embracing Oneness with Tao and Consciousness," introduces a number of important practical concepts, beginning with the union of vitality and consciousness. The text speaks of concentration, flexibility, purification of insight, naturalness, being innocent, acting without presumption: all of these came to be regarded as critical elements of Taoist spirituality in both the science of essence and the science of life (Cleary, 1987; Wing, 1986; Clarke, 1994, 2000).

Tao teaching employs both rational and intuitive consciousness: as the text says, "To perceive the small is called insight. To remain yielding is called strength. In using one's brightness one returns to insight" (Tao Te Ching in Wing, 1986, Chapter 52). These illustrate how ordinary faculties of the human mind are subordinated to the higher faculty of the mind of Tao without being debased or broken (Wing, 1986). "The richness of subliminal virtue" (Tao Te Ching in Wing, 1986, Chapter fifty-five), metaphorically describes ideal combinations of flexibility and firmness, innocence and empowerment. The chapter also presents the key concepts of mastering energy by mind and sustaining power by restraint.

When externals do not confuse you inwardly, your nature finds the condition that suits it. Human nature is generally such that it likes tranquility and dislikes anxiety; it likes leisure and dislikes toil. When the spirit controls the body, the body obeys; when the body overrules the spirit, the spirit is exhausted. Although intelligence is useful, it needs to be returned to the spirit. This is called the unity and harmony (Wing, 1986). "Return to the Nature" (Lau, 1992), the spirit of the storehouse of awareness will return to the beginning of myriad things. They look at the formless, listen to the soundless. In the midst of profound darkness, they alone see light. They live through death. In the midst of silent vastness, they alone have discernment free from seductive longings, and energy and will are open and calm. Then it is not difficult to see the precedents, to see the connections to the past and the aftermath of the future (Richards, 1989).

Tao directs attention towards the psychological, aesthetic, and spiritual realm, often neglected dimensions of life. Grigg (1999) stresses that "...will find the New Lao-tzu a recognizable element of Zen. Indeed, the special psychological and philosophical forces that constitute one are also the essential qualities of the other" (p. 150). He continues say,

> Tao, like Zen, is not a philosophy of life; it is the art of being. Like the artistic process itself, Taoism embraces all the inherent contradictions of living, and then it converts the creative energy that result from this tension into a balancing and harmonizing experience. (p. 114)

The art of living cultivates emotional inner peace, appreciation of the beauty and experience of life in itself, and an orientation towards the source and unity of life and being which transcends the petty problems of the world and the institutions of society. He/she sought to clarify the inner dimensions of the self and the spiritual dimensions of the world. The experience of the Tao is analogous to the creativity of the artist and aesthetic appreciation of the observer. The art of living cultivates the unity of life in its dynamic flux (Chang, 1963; Rowley, 1955).

With infinite empty space, Tao can absorb the different worlds of psychology and art, different religions and the many others ways (Chang, 1963, pp. 1-15).  Psychological theories provide detailed information on the formation of the self.  Tao gives an insight into the direction and framework.  Chang (1963) notes,

> Never before has Chinese Tao Te Ching been so well explained in the light of modern psychology and sincerely pursued as a way to elevate man's mental activities and alleviate his sufferings. Thus mystery of age-old Eastern wisdom, which brings out the best in man, is no longer a mystery but simply a way to wholesome and harmonious living. (p. 6)

To search for the meaning of self is a lifelong learning process.  The central role of the self is able to turn happenings into meanings (Spence, 1987).  From psychotherapy to spirituality, the Tao of living cultivates emotional inner peace.  Although ignorance and pain exist, spirituality suggests that suffering and death are included, and eventually transcend the greater whole, which preserves us, and – however impersonally – wishes us well. Sometimes we experience ourselves as isolated; but by sharing human experience vertically (inward) and horizontally (outward), we could discover that we are participants in a large and meaningful whole.  A person comes to know his/her position between heaven and earth.  As a 'co-creator' he/she breakthroughs his/her boundary, embraces paradox with wisdom and works toward change and transformation.  Finally, he/she finds meaning in life by "passing on" these experiences.

# IV   ART: TRUTH, LOVE, AND BEAUTY

My clinic is like a gallery, a game room and a stage of life. It is a safe place where my clients can share their experiences and discover themselves in a deeper senses. Through arts, I echo with my client's life experiences.  All feelings and human characters are honestly revealed and safely revealed in this sacred space.   There are laughter, tears, griefs, sadness, disappointment, hope, cynicism, irritability, depression, trauma, convulsions, anxiety, confusion, direction and confidence… Life has given us scratches and we transform them into in an artistic light and beauty. I want to thank everyone who met in my studio and they are precious in my life journey.  Every moment is eternal in the contact between lives.  (For respect privacy, all the names in case studies are false name.)

我是一個心理治療師，辦公室不像醫務所，倒像是畫廊、 遊戲室、又像一個人生舞台。每天我就在這兒與相遇的人經歷生命。裡面有歡笑聲、悲痛、哭泣、茫然、失望、希望、憤世嫉俗、激怒、憂傷、鬱結、創傷、驚惶失措、焦慮、疑惑、方向、信心…種種情懷、人性真實地顯露無遺。生命給我們傷痛，我們可以將它編織成美麗的圖畫及詩篇。我是有福的能夠與相遇的人坦蕩蕩地對談生命的點滴， 這是我的榮幸，每一刻都是永恒。（為尊重私隱，案主名字都是假名。）

# 馴 獸 師

## *Animal Trainer*

小個子的<u>毅忠</u>怒忽忽的走入遊戲室的繪畫角，很快的繪畫了一幅飛機大炮的戰爭場面，繼而他想用紙製造一立體飛機模型。七歲的<u>毅忠</u>是家庭暴力的受害者，父母正辦理離婚手續。

他每星期接受心理治療一次，以上的兩個情節是他每次『執著地』必要做的活動環節，並會用一卷透明膠紙將立體飛機模型黏得牢牢之後他才肯罷休，這正表達了毅忠內心的焦慮不安，忿怒, 這是我所明白和理解的。正當我躊躇著是否要阻止他每次用一整卷膠紙時，我靈機一觸對他說：「我明白你很想把父母的問題處理得完完整整，但離婚的事是成人的決定，已經成為事實，你怎樣將飛機貼得牢牢的，也不能改變。但我相信他們對你的愛是不變的！」

<u>毅忠</u>聽後哭成淚人。我安撫他的憂傷和疑慮，半年後，<u>毅忠</u>將他的『執著』正面地放在『馴獸師』的角色轉換遊戲上。他說：「我要做一個馴獸師，不讓它們（動物）傷害人。」

Yi Chung, a 7-year-old boy, was a victim of domestic violence.  His parents were in the process of divorce.  This angry little boy run into the playroom and started painting. His painting was a scene of war aircraft, and then he wanted to create a three-dimensional paper model aircraft. He insisted to have the above two activities each session. He would use a roll of transparent tape for the three-dimensional plane model. Not until he felt that the paper plane was firmly stuck, he would not give up.  This might reveal Yi Chung's inner anxiety and insecurity.  A thought came into me when I tried to stop him using up a full roll of tape.  I gently said to him: "I understand what you really want is to fix parents' divorce. But the divorce thing is the decision of adults, has become a reality.  No matter how firm you try to tape the aircraft, you cannot change it.  But, I believe their love to you does not change! " Upon hearing my word, Yi Chung's rolled down from his face. Six months later, Yi Chung dedicated to his role being an animal trainer. A positive role is placed on the change game. He said: "I want to be a trainer, I don't let them (animals) hurt people."

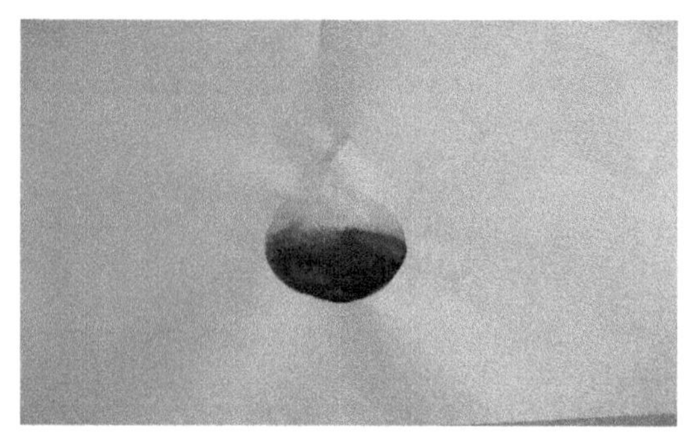

# 生命是一個逗號、不是句號
## *Life is not a Full Stop*

嵐風剛過十七歲生日，她對人生感到絕望，曾企圖自殺！卻又希望完美無瑕地追尋生命的意義；她極賦藝術才華，卻看不起自己的作品，她力求完美，又覺得自己不如別人。嵐風每天浸淫於完美的假象中，給自己極大的壓力，常處於惶恐中，並覺得一舉一動被人監視。

經歷多月來的心理治療後，與此同時，嵐風獲得最著名學府的取錄。在她出國讀書前，她畫了這幅發人深省的畫。我對她的描述拍案叫絕。

「人生不是一個句號，是逗號。這個逗號可從兩面觀看。黑、灰、白構成這一逗點。 黑色是人生的痛苦灰暗面，白色是夢想，灰色地帶是夢想的橋樑，痛苦的沉殿；掉過頭來看，也是提升，白色的尾巴藉著灰色的導航向夢想飛去，不斷地延伸，生生不息。」

這是完美!

Lan Feng just celebrated her 17 years old birthday.  She felt despair of life and had suicidal thoughts!  She hope to have a perfect way to pursue the meaning of life.  In spite of her highly artistic talent, she looked down on her own artworks. Strived for perfection, she also felt inferior. Immersed in the illusion of perfectionism, she put tremendous pressure on herself.  She was often in fears: and she felt that was being watched of her every move.

After many months of treatment, Lan Feng passed the entrance examination of the most famous institute. Before she went to study, she painted a piece of thought-provoking paintings. I found her lovely description:

*"Life is not a full stop, but is a comma.  This comma can be watched from both sides.  This comma is composed of black, grey and white. Black is a dark side of life's hardships, white is a dream, grey areas is a bridge from pain to dream.  Turn around the comma and it has another point of view: the white tail rises up, and it flies toward the dream through the grey's navigation.  It is extended continuously.  It prospers endlessly. "*

This is perfect!

黑 中 有 白 、 白 中 有 黑

## Black and White

勇兒八歲的時候，目睹家庭暴力，以及父親被警察帶走。父親是社區一個出色的公眾人物，他心裡面對極大的衝擊。勇兒在學校裡變得沉默寡言，鬱鬱不樂，學業一落千丈，有時更有攻擊性行為。然而，在家裡卻很聽話與合作，答應母親任何的要求。

在沙箱治療 (Sand Box) 中，勇兒多次將黑白沙混在一起。 在他入神地攪拌著泥沙的時候，我對他說： ""「你一定不能理解與接受父親兩種相反的性格(好與壞)同時存在。黑沙與白沙混在一起反映著你內心的矛盾。" 勇兒皺著眉頭看了我一眼，又繼續玩沙。我再說： ""「真的，人生有時是黑中有白，白中有黑，分不清楚。就如你對父親的感覺：又愛又恨！你對父親的忠心，愛他的感情是正確的；而你恨他的行為也是正確的。這兩種感情是可以同時存在的。我們要學習接受後，才懂得選擇不重複父親的行為。」

勇兒經歷一年的療程，他學習將內心的矛盾以適當的行為表達出來。另一方面，在學校裡也慢慢地投入學習，並再展笑顏。

Yong, an eight year-old boy, witnessed domestic violence and his father was taken away by police on the spot.  It was hard for Yong to understand and to accept about his father, who was a great community public figure, and yet he did such things at home. Yong became quiet in school.   He was depressed and unhappy.  Academic was plummeted.  He sometimes had aggressive behavior towards students.  Nevertheless, Yong was very obedient and cooperative at home.  He agreed to his mother's any demands.

Treatment in the sandbox, Yong repeatedly mixed black and white sand. He was engrossed in stirring the sand, I said: "You must not understand and accept that your father of two opposing personalities (good and bad) together. Black sand mixed with white sand reflects your inner contradictions." Yong frowned and looked at me, but continued to play sand. I said: "Really, life is sometimes black in white, white in black, poorly demarcated.  Just as how you feel ── love and hate your father at the same time! Your loyalty and love towards your father is inborn; and your hateful feelings are correct. These two feelings can co-exist. We should learn to accept that before we know how to choose not to repeat father's behavior."  Yong went through a year of treatment. He was brave to accept his inner conflicts and learned to express in appropriate behavior. Slowly, he was able to put his energy back to study.

# 葬 禮

## *Buried my Grandfather*

九歲的 Flamenco 回菲律賓奔喪，送別爺爺的最後一程。回到加拿大後，心神焦慮，常坐立不安和失眠。被確診為過度活躍症 (A.D. H .D.)。父母對藥物治療存疑信參半。Flamenco 接受十次療程後，生活回復正常，失眠也沒有了。 Flanaco 在沙箱治療中不停的將葬禮重現，並呈現非常驚惶失措的樣子，自言自語急促地說：「爺爺被葬埋入泥土，那裡有很多蟲子，他會被吃掉! 為甚麼？為甚麼他會被遺棄在那裡？他一定感到冰冷又孤零零。我很害怕，怕有一天我也會被掉在那裡？怎麼辦呢？…」

當兒童面對死亡，無論是接觸語言、文字、視像、抑或親身的經驗，對他們來說，很多時都會帶來一連串的疑惑和震撼。Flamenco 反映的情緒行為是可理解的，而不是過度活躍症。我們要小心識別和處理。此時，治療師可以安撫兒童的情緒，把情緒正常化，並解釋死亡的意義。我們要設身處地，以孩子的心態與他們溝通。我會這樣解釋：

「死亡就是說再見的意思。我們每天都常常與朋友說再見，但明天還會與朋友再見面；早上跟家人說再見，但晚上會再回到家中與家人見面。而死亡只是較長時間的再見，將來我們可與那親人在天家再見面的！」

Flamenco went back to the Philippines to attend his grandfather's funeral. He exhibited anxious mind, restless, and insomnia after returning to Canada. Flamenco was diagnosed with hyperactivity disorder (A.D.H.D). Parents doubted about the use of drug treatment. Flamenco returned his normal life after received ten art therapy sessions.

In the sandbox, Flamenco did not stop to reproduce the funeral episode, and showed a very panic-stricken expression. He said: "Grandpa is buried in the soil which has a lot of insects. He will be eaten! Why is he abandoned there? He must have felt cold and lonely. I am afraid, One day I will be thrown down there too. How can it be?  What can I do? "

Flamenco reflecting the emotional insecurity was understandable, but it was not hyperactivity behavior. The therapist normalized and acknowledged his emotions, feelings, and explained: "Death is to say Good-bye. Every day we say goodbye to friends, but we will meet them again the next day.  We say goodbye to our family in the morning, but we will see them again when we come home at night. Death is just a long-time Goodbye; we will see our loved ones again in heaven or somewhere in space.

## 不 一 樣 的 智 慧 與 愛

### *Different Kind of Wisdom & Love*

十八歲的忠庸自幼被評估為自閉兒，但他極賦音樂天份，考取了十級鋼琴程度。他沉默寡言，有社交困難，言語上只限於一問一答的簡單應對，極少長篇大論。他每次來到我的畫室，祇要求讓他靜靜地繪畫；一邊繪畫，一邊聽他喜愛的ＣＤ，他雖不懂書寫中文，但他却愛聽中文流行歌曲，如李克勤、張學友、許冠文等的歌，他都能一一詠唱。有時他會要求我為他的畫寫下中文註解.

中學畢業後，他進讀大學並接受職業訓練。有一天，他如常地繪畫，不一樣的是，他對我說他在學校裏認識了一位女朋友，並詳盡地跟我述說他的計畫：「我愛她! 我給她兩星期考慮是否願意成為我的女朋友。我是有特殊需要，因此我不會找到好好的工作。但我會找一份穩定工作，我們就結婚。」

很多時候，自閉兒常被父母或眾人評定為思想行徑不正常的人，然而，在忠庸身上，世人的眼光理應重新調整和改變。

18-year-old Chung-yung was diagnosed with autism when he was a child.  However, he was very talented in music.  He passed the level 10 piano at his young age. He was quiet and had social difficulties with speech delay. Every time he came to my studio, and requested to paint quietly. He painted while listening to his favorite Chinese CD. Though he did not know written Chinese, he liked to listen Chinese pop songs.

After graduating from high school, he entered university vocational training. One day, he painted in the same manner; he told the therapist that he met a girl in school.  And he expressed his detail plans: "I love her and I give her two weeks to think about whether or not she wants to be my girlfriend.  I am a special need.  I will not find a good job. But I will get a job, and then we can get marry. "

In many cases, autistic children are often perceived to act abnormally.  However, we should re-adjust our definition of Autism with Chung-yung's wisdom and love.

# 我 沮 喪 的 心
## *Depressed Heart*

這是我沮喪的心，沒有希望。它充滿汙土，沒有甚麼能填充其中！我尋找生活的意義，我期望有光引領。

我看見十字架，但它是苦澀和痛苦的。 有時十字架的大能減輕我的痛苦，但我仍需背負和承擔這痛苦的十架。 我找不到活水的泉源！

我外表是非常愉快的，像藍天般晴朗，但內裏卻有很多大大小小的石塊。起初，我以為通過分享可把它們挪走。可是，隨著時間過去， 我發覺石塊變成灰色了！

我發現，在我周遭，也有很多抑鬱的人。為什麼我必須背負他們的擔子？我要學習分辨責任及將不屬於自己的交給天父。 我也應學習對我所作的事情不寄予厚望，那我會比預期中做得更好

This is my heart - depressed and hopeless. It is full of polluted soil. Nothing could fill it!  I am looking for the meaning of life. I see the cross, but it is bitter and painful.  Sometimes the power of the cross reduces my pain, but I still need to carry and bear the pains of the cross.  I cannot find the fountain of living waters!

My appearance is very pleasant like the clear blue sky, but it actually had many obstacles in my heart. At first, I thought by sharing them, they can be moved away.

However, over time, those obstacles turned grey! I find many depressed people around me. Why do I have to carry their burden?  I need to have a clear mind and learn to discern what is my responsibility and what is not.  I also need to learn to do things without too much expectation. Then, I would do better.

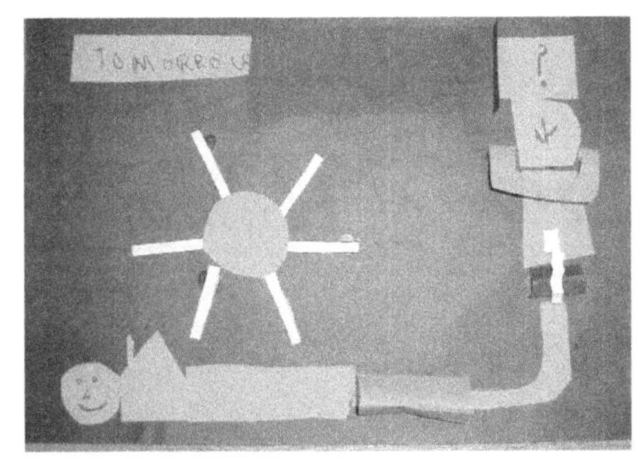


# 我 不 知 明 天 的 光 景

## *I Don't Know About Tomorrow*

踏入壯年才失業，使黃先生突然間失去一份安全感與信心，並患上了憂鬱焦慮症。參加醫院精神科外診部藝術治療小組活動時，他以手工紙剪貼出一幅很有意義的圖畫：

> 「我看不見明天，前面祇是一條漆黑的隧道，我鼓起勇氣向前行
> 走，不知隧道中有甚麼，走出隧道後，看見一個山洞路障，我繼
> 續穿越，又遇見一座階梯，也擋住了視線，看不見前路，但我仍
> 努力往上爬；後來有一條平路，繼續前行並再通過另一條隧道，
> 我終於看見一幢房屋。房屋內有人以笑臉歡迎我，也看見太陽耀
> 眼的光彩普照著！」

Experiencing layoff in the prime of life, Mr. Wong found it difficult to face his sudden lost.  He lost a sense of security and confidence.  He suffered from depression and anxiety.  Mr. Wong participated in Psychiatric outpatient art therapy group activities.  He handed in a meaningful artwork:

*"I cannot see tomorrow in front of a dark tunnel. I take courage to walk forward. I do not know what is in the tunnel. Out of a tunnel cave, I see a roadblock. I continue to go through. Then I see a ladder. I climb up, but the view of the road is still blocked. I still try hard to climb upwards. Then there is a flat road. I keep going and pass through another tunnel. I finally see a house. People in the house welcome me with big smiles. And I see the sun shine with dazzling brilliance!"*

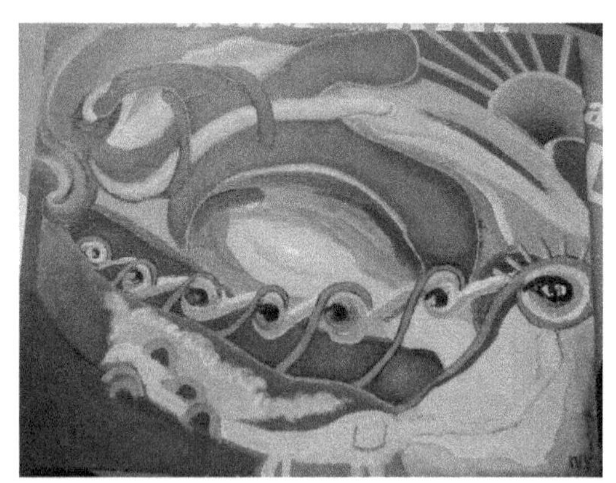

# 人 的 本 質
## *Essence of Human*

一個飽受精神困擾及心靈創傷的少女，她告訴我最能令她安靜和滿足的是觀看造物者的創造，她感覺安全與平安。當一個人與永恆不變的造物主相遇時， 無論怎樣的創傷也變得很微不足道，因為這些烙印都不能傷害到人的本質：

我是一個有用的、

有價值的、

值得愛的、

有建設性的人啊！

Senling said,

*"I am contemplating God's creation. I feel content and peaceful.  I am loved by God."*

When someone encounters with God, our wounds will diminish. Because no one can

hurt the human essence that God gives us.

I am capable

I am worthy

I am loved

I am constructive

# 邪 惡 的 心
# *The Evil Heart*

我認為人之初，善惡都存在於我們的裡面；看這幅畫：用各種毒藥製造的蛋糕，是用來送給老師的！

Ming 笑著對我說：「我恨我的老師！」

我問他：「你知這樣做，有甚麼後果嗎？」「當然知道啦，所以我用繪畫來表示出來。我喜歡畫畫，是因可以把沒辦法做的事實現出來，而又不會傷害到別人。」

「邪惡」只是愛的欠缺！我們要讓兒童學習在善與惡之間作出警覺性的選擇.

I believe good and evil both exist in human nature.  Look at this picture: a cake made with poisons--a gift for teacher!

Ming smiled and said, *"I hate my teacher! Hee Hee Hee!"*

I asked him: "Do you know the consequences of doing this?" "

*"Of course, I know the matter, so I express it with drawings. I like drawing. I get my way out without harming others. "*

"Evil" is just a lack of love! We teach children to make good choice between good and evil vigilantly.

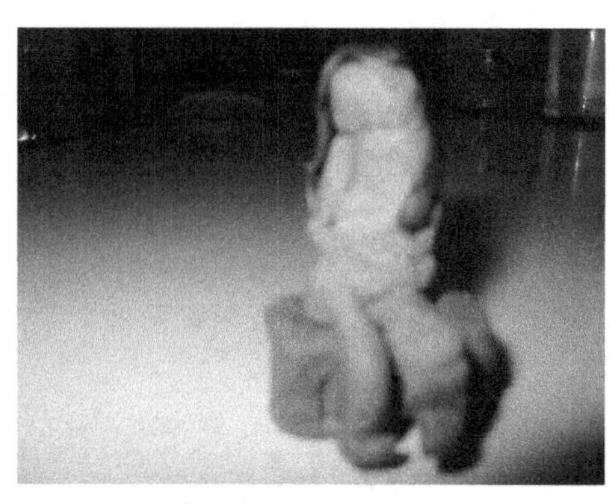

# 不 能 飛 的 女 孩
## *Girl Cannot Fly!*

「我母親是虔誠的基督徒，我們每晚都要在一起禱告，我們不願意，她便會不開心，破口大罵。」

「她這樣做，妳感覺不到她的愛，是嗎？」

「她雖說很愛我，但我一點也感受不到。爸爸是「太空人」（註），又不在身邊。他雖買了很多東西給我，但我最想的只是一家人在一起吃一頓飯。」

「沒有被愛的感覺，使妳動彈不得？」

「是呀！就像這小女孩。」

「可否多告訴我一些關於這小女孩的事？」

「她很憂傷，很想死！又很恐懼考不進大學，她想擺脫母親，但她不能飛。」

（註）「太空人」 是指沒有太太和家人在身旁，在定人定居的地方與工作的地方不斷往返的丈夫。太空家庭製造了很多家庭問題，如婚姻出軌、子女成長失去方向等等，都嚴重地破壞家庭的和諧。

"Mother is a devoted Christian. We pray every night together. If we are not willing, she will be unhappy and yell at us."

*"You don't feel her love for you."*

"She says she loves me. I do not feel that. Father is not around us.  Although he bought a lot expensive things for me, I just want to have one meal with him. "

*"There is no feeling of being loved, so that you could not fly? "*

"Yes! Like this little girl."

*"Tell me more about this little girl."*

"She is sad. She wants to die!  She wants to leave her mother, but she cannot fly away."

# 生命與死亡
# *Life and Death*

相對於的死亡，生是幸福的。相對於生命，死是和平的
生，並不一定是幸福! 死，並不一定是可悲的
愛是藏於心底，但未必能表達出來
沒有愛，我們的心感覺空虛
缺乏自信，是一種無形的傷疤
太多的愛，我們的心感到麻痺
不知道如何欣賞和驕傲
事實上，生與死，是不在我們控制之下
我們所能做的是活在當下
對我們自己的使命和工作負責、並好好享受人生
愛是與生俱來的，愛展現在相互的關係中
愛需要培養和耐心，所以，你知道什麼是愛
你就可以愛了。
愛是我們的本性，但不是必然的
你未必懂得如何以愛還愛
生命是一個漫長曲折的道路
如果我能與我的摯愛同行到底
我不會後悔此生了。


Relative to death, life is happy. Relative to life, death is peaceful. Life, not necessarily happy.
Death, not necessarily sad. Love is hidden in your heart, but, not necessarily expressed.
Without love, our heart feels empty. Lack of confidence, is an invisible scar.
Too much love, our heart feels paralyze. Do not know how to appreciate and be arrogant.
In fact, life and death are out of our control
All we can do is to live in the present
Responsible for our own mission – to work, to enjoy…
Love is inborn,  Love reveal in relationship
Love need nurture and patience
Therefore, you know what is love
And, you can love
Love is our nature, but
Not necessary you know how to return in love
Life is a long winding road
If I can walk with my love to the end
I will have no regrets in life.

# 馬 塞 克 的 人 生
## Life of Mosaic

黃太太一邊把紙張撕碎，一邊思量著如何整合這些看起來像垃圾的紙碎。黃太很用心的將一塊一塊的碎紙拼貼，她說：「我花了幾個星期的時間才能拼貼出這朵我最喜愛的蓮花。本來，是用不著這麼長時間的，但當我在拼拼貼貼時，每想到我的人生也像那些紙碎，心靈被多次撕碎，我便要停頓下來，不能再拼湊下去！」

她繼續說：「我思量過去曾經歷過的創傷，都未能將我的人生毀壞掉，於是我便有勇氣重新拿起膠水，繼續用心的拼貼下去，整合成這美麗的花朵。」

我帶著微笑並對她說：「好！我也認為這是屬於妳的美麗花朵。」

Mrs. Wong tore the paper up into pieces, as she pondered how to work with these garbage-like pieces of paper.  She was keen to put pieces of shredded paper into a collage.

She said: *"I spent a few weeks to put these shredded pieces of paper together and formed my favorite lotus flower. Originally, it should not have taken such a long time.  However, when I worked on collage, I thought of my life just like those pieces of paper.  My heart has been torn apart into pieces.  When those memories came, I had to stop. I could not rig it up!"*

She continued: *"Then, I pondered upon my past traumatic experiences, and saw that they could not destroy my life.  So, I picked up the courage re-glue this collage, attentively to integrate the paper pieces into the beautiful flowers."*

I smiled and said to her: "Good! I also think that this beautiful flower belongs to you."

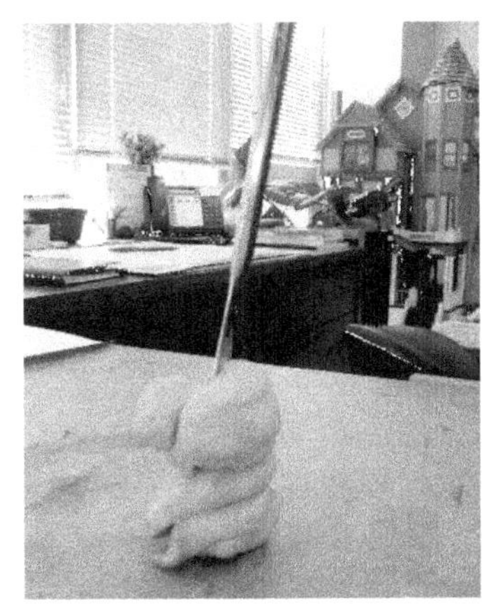

# 一 歲 的 記 憶

## One Year Old Memory

若您以為嬰孩是沒有記憶的，那您就錯了！事實上，兩歲前的經歷都會深深地留在潛意識世界裏。七歲的<u>恆輝</u>整天眨眼、坐立不定、失眠，在校常騷擾同學，這些症狀已有多時，還被精神科醫生診斷為焦慮症，除了用藥，苦無對策。

<u>恆輝</u>接受了約一年的藝術治療，有一天，他用黏土塑造了一個人型，突然間，他拿起黏土刀插在塑像的頭上，他說：「我好像記得爸媽有一天吵架，突然間，有一東西擲在媽媽的頭上，她就倒下來死了！我不知這是不是夢？」

作為一個心理治療師，深知這一情景終會出現，我並不感愕然，平靜地對他說：「這不是夢境，是你一歲半前的記憶。媽媽雖然死了，她如今在天堂，你無需再恐懼、不安，媽媽會保守你的。」

這個案是較複雜，隨後<u>恆輝</u>再接受半年的心理輔導，他焦慮的行為減少了，在校生活有所改善並投入正常的學習。

Baby has memory! In fact, the first two years of experience remain deeply in the subconscious world.  Hang Fai, a 7-year-old boy, blinked his eyes all day.  He was restless and had insomnia.  He constantly harassed his school friends.  He was diagnosed with anxiety disorder and ADHD with medication for many years.

Hang Fai received a year of art therapy treatment. One day, he created a human figure with clay.  Suddenly, he put a knife into the head of the clay person. He said: *"I kind of remember that the day my parents fought.  One thing was thrown at my mother's head suddenly.  She fell down and died! I do not know if this is a dream or not? "*

As a psychotherapist, I am well aware of this scenario will eventually occur.  I am not stunned, but gently said to him: "This is not a dream. It is your memory when you were one year old.  Although your mother is dead, she is now in heaven.  You need not afraid and feel anxious.  Your mother protects you all the time. "

Hang Fai had difficulty to accept the fact that his mother was dead.  After he realized that it was not a dream, his anxiety was reduced.  Finally, he overcome and accepted the fact.

# 痛 苦 藏 骨 髓
## *Pains in My Bones*

她述說：「那痛苦感覺是如此強烈，就像自己的骨頭在互相拷打和撕裂一樣，使我心緒不定，坐立不安。」她繼續：「我很想停止這場爭戰，但好像死在幽暗中！」
我說：「那是你的骨頭在爭戰，我相信你很想拒絕它們，想將這些骨頭推出身體之外。」

她對應道：「也許是吧！理性上知道對父親是沒有選擇，但在感性上若他不是我父親……」

「那怎麼辨呢？」
後來給她繪畫了一幅「被醫治的骨頭」。
圖畫中表達了畫者得到上帝愛的滋潤與光照，那屬於她的骨骼可得到醫治。

She said: *"It's such a strong feeling! The pain is like the bones colliding and tearing at each other. It is a torture. I am in an uncertain state of mind, restless."* She continued: *"I would like to stop this war! "*

I said: "Your bones are at war. I believe you want to reject it, and would like to repel these bones outside your body."

She responded: *"I suppose so! Rationally I know that I have to accept my father. There is no choice!"*

"So, what can you do? "

In other session, she painted a picture "Heal the bones". She expressed the picture was painted in the light of God's tender love. The power healed her pains.

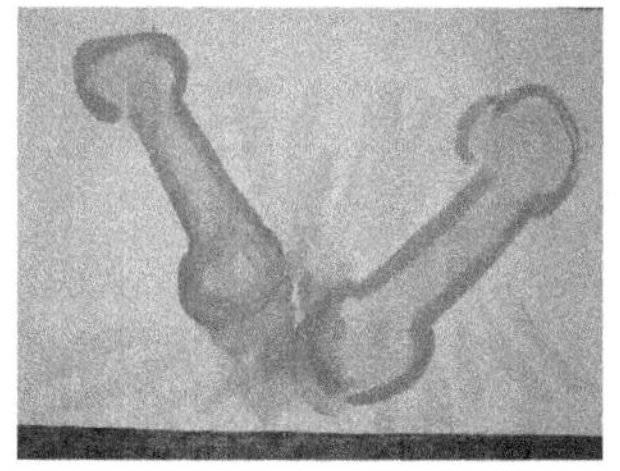

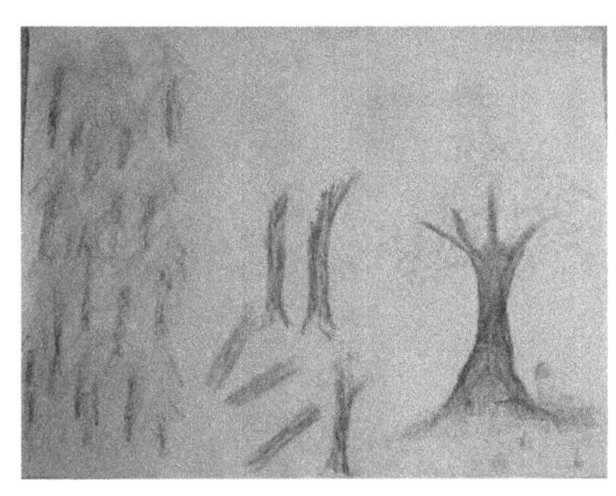

# 過 去 ， 現 在 ， 將 來
## *Past, Present, Future*

過去我在森林裡迷失了，樹是枯乾的並且逐漸死去！但現在樹再重生成為鳥兒的家。我感謝上帝使我曾經歷過憂鬱，我的生命就像那些樹，死而復生。瞭解到人生需要與大自然和上帝有一個復和的關係，必須學做一個忠誠的人。我曾經認為生活只是受苦，現在我想要慶祝和享有生活。

我曾是一個非常被動和馴服的人，滿足任何人的要求。現在，學會跟隨我的意志。同時，我是愉快的，其他人也是愉快的。

現在，我有勇氣表達我的想法。 我曾經在丈夫面前不敢談論我的需要，現在，我可以建議其他方法或使用更好的表達能力談論我的需要。 我不想損害我丈夫的感覺，另一方面，我也不壓抑自己，學會了不執著，懂得愛惜自己。

In the past, I got lost in the forest, where the trees were gradually withered and died!  Now the trees are reborn to be homes for birds.  I thank God that I had experienced depression. My life is like the trees, reborn from death.  I understand life needs to be having a reconciled relationship within God and nature.  We must learn to be a loyal person.  I used to think that life is just a suffering, and now I want to celebrate and rejoice in life.

I was very passive and docile people who want to meet the demands of any person.  Now, I learn to follow my will.  I and other people are happy at the same time.

Now, I have the courage to express my thoughts. In front of my husband, I was not able to talk about my needs.  Now, I can recommend other ways or use better communication skills to express my needs.  I do not want to hurt my husband's feelings.  On the other hand, I do not suppress my own needs.  I learn not to detach myself, but know how to love myself.

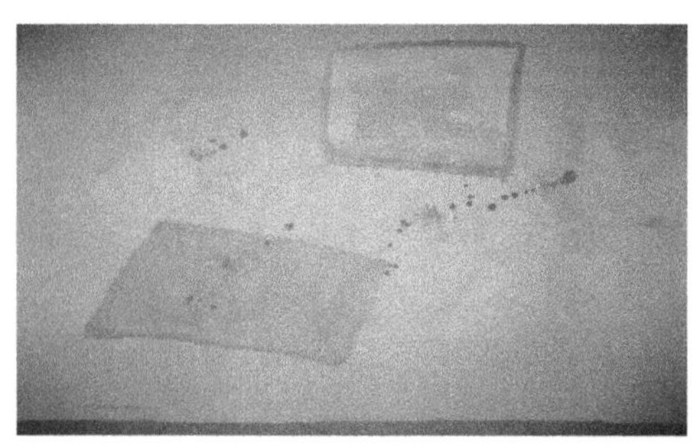

# 峰 迴 路 轉
## The Turning Point

在療程停滯不前時，當遇上峰迴路轉，我心是雀躍萬分。因我也經歷到當事人生命成長的一刻，是何等的珍貴與喜悅。這份經驗不是別人可拿走的，也不是金錢可買得。

十七歲的嵐風墮入生的黑洞，徘徊自殺邊緣多年。這幾個月來，我與她在畫中經歷死蔭的幽谷。這天她大膽豪放地繪畫這幅畫。她描述：「灰色長方形是理性的框架，將痛苦扭曲的思維和情緒歸納於其中。藍色的框架有綠色的光明和希望。紅點是跳躍的喜悅橫跨黑暗與光明。」我喜出望外地凝視著著這幅畫說：「好! 好! 好!令人拍案叫絕！」

嵐風繼續說：「我學會了分辨負面與正面的思維，並學習為光明作出決定。」

我說：「這是很珍貴的發現。」

嵐風笑著說：「我想擁有這永恆。」

我回應並問：「妳不是擁有了嗎？妳想只擁有一幅畫，
還是人生擁有很多幅畫？」

她雀躍地說：「我明白、人生不在乎擁有，而是經歷。」

我會心微笑地問：「妳能畫同一幅畫嗎？」

嵐風也笑了：「那已是不一樣了。我不想緬懷過去。」

我拍拍她的肩膀說：「Well Done!」

In the course of stagnation, when my client took a dramatic turn, I was overjoying.  How precious it is to share my clients' life experience moments.  It is priceless and cannot be taken away.

Lan Feng, a 17-year-old girl, once fell into the black hole of her life.  She had been wandering on the edge of suicide for many years.  For a few months, we experienced "Valley-of-the-shallow-of-death" together.  Today she is bold to paint this picture. She described: "grey rectangle is a rational framework for the twisted thoughts and painful feelings.  Blue frame with green light is hope.  Red dots are the joy jumping across the dark and light."

I gazed at the picture with a pleasant surprise: *"Well! Good! Good!"*

Lan Feng went on to say: "I learned how to distinguish between negative and positive thinking, as well as making bright decision."  I said: *"This is a very valuable discovery."*

Lan Feng said with a smile: "I want this moment to last forever."

I responded and asked: *"Haven't you possessed it already?  Do you only want to have one picture in your life? Or life fills with a lot of beautiful paintings?"*

She was delighted and said: "I know!  Life is not about possession, but experiences."

I asked with smile: *"Can you paint the same painting?"*

Lan Feng smiled: "It is no longer the same. I do not hold on to the past."

I patted her shoulder and said: *"Well done!"*

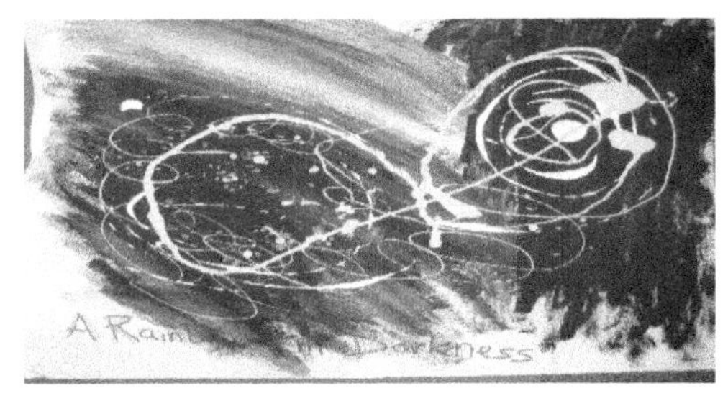

# 黑　暗　中　的　彩　虹

## *Rainbow in the Darkness*

浩然與弟弟常被父親肢體和情緒虐待。當父母打架很厲害時，他們會躲在漆黑的衣櫃裏，他覺得黑暗有安全感，卻未曾察覺這是恐懼感。慢慢他常感到沮喪、憂鬱，做事欠缺動力，只喜歡靜悄悄的躲在房間或沉迷於電子遊戲機裡，他社交生活有困難。

他告訴我：「我喜歡與網友聊天，他們是我真正的朋友，學校的人不是我朋友，他們令我感到害怕！」

他畫了一幅「黑暗」，我建議他在上面加上光明，也一面跟他討論光明在黑暗中會更顯得明亮，光明會勝過黑暗。而光明的來源就是「愛與關懷」

經過一段日子，浩然才能走出黑暗的角落，投入學習與認識新朋友。

When their parents fought, Noble and his brother would hide inside the dark closet.  Noble felt secured in the dark.  He expressed that he liked evil and wanted to be evil.  As a result, he was depressed, and lost the motivation to do things.  He just liked to hide in his quiet room or indulged in video games.  He had difficulty in his social life.

Noble told me: *"I like to chat with friends on the Internet.  They are my true friends.  People at school are not my friends.  They make me feel scared!"*

He drew a painting called "Darkness" and said, *"I am evil."*  I said gently, *"Evil is not terrible. It is just lack of love. They don't have power."*  I suggested him to add yellow on top of the dark.  And I said, *"The darker it is, the brighter it will be."*  We discussed about the bright side and the dark side of life.  The root of light source was: "Love and Care".  Then, he added a rainbow on the top.

After some time, Noble and his brother got out of their dark corners. They turned their energy into learning and making new friends.

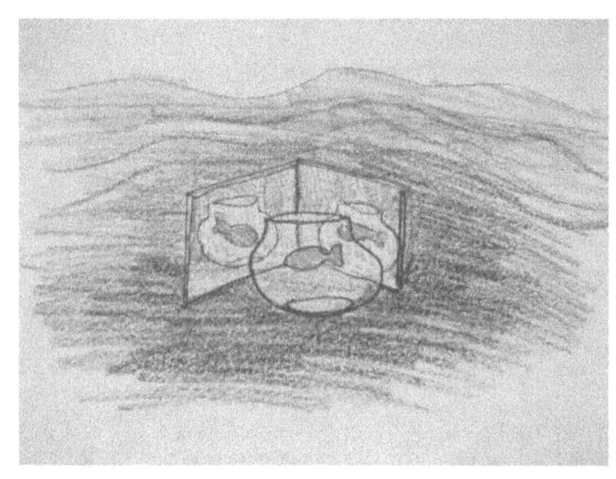

# 時 間 是 很 重 要
## *Time is Important*

個案主角為一移民加拿大的中年人仕，過著休閒的退休生活，在沒想到經濟壓力下卻患上「恐慌症」，做了數次的藝術治療，他像茅塞頓開，發現了令他恐慌的根源。以下是其中一次的對話：

「我發現時間是如此重要，我學會了看最重要的事情。當我聽到有關新聞、經濟、政治……我試圖找出哪些是最重要的事情。首先，我會略去那不重要的事情。」

*「充份利用寶貴時間，有效率地用在重要的事情上是一件好事。但請留心聽，我想問你一個問題——**你有沒有自己的時間呢？** 還是給所有的時間都耗在政治、暴力新聞、財經新聞上呢？」*

他默默點頭，答：「是的，我從來沒有想到這一點。這是一個很好的提醒，我需要去考慮這個問題。」

*「好！下次告訴我你的經驗吧。」*

A middle-aged man immigrated to Canada for his retirement.  Despite with his economic security, he suffered from "panic disorder" unexpectedly.  He came for several art therapy sessions.  He was enlightened and discovered his root of fears.

 The following was one of our dialogues:
"I found that time is so important. When I heard of the news about economic, political situations... I'm trying to find out what is the most important thing. First, I would eliminate things that are not important. "

*"Full use of valuable time, efficient use for the important things is a good habit. Nevertheless, please listen carefully, I would like to ask you a question —— Do you have your own time?  Or instead, you spend all of the time on political, financial, violence news."*

He silently nodded and replied: "Yes, I have never thought of that. This is a good reminder. I need to consider this issue."

*"Good! Next time, share with me your experience how to use your time for yourself. Thanks."*

# 媽 媽 的 微 笑

## *Mom's Smiling Face*

五歲的靖靖母親患上乳癌，目睹母親在過去一年接受放射性治療，在絕望和死亡的邊緣，掙扎求生，後戰勝了病魔，母親的勇敢與正面積極的態度，使靖靖學習到在危難中藉著信念和希望，接受外在的支援，如心理輔導或其他社會資源，終能渡過難關。

這是一正面和積極的生存態度，被標籤為精神病的患者，其起因除了遺傳因子外，若他/她祇會固步自封，不懂尋求外援或不肯接受別人幫助，亦沒有適當地處理情緒，那大多會走入問題的黑洞和絕望中！

靖靖與母親一起經歷難關，悲喜交集，有恐懼徬徨的階段，但最後仍能在她的沙畫上畫上笑臉，演繹出她所體會到的新生命和希望。

Jing Jing, a 5-year-old girl, whose mother suffered, had breast cancer.  She witnessed her mother's suffering because of radiotherapy in the past year.  On the edge of despair and death, her mother struggled to survive.  Finally, she had victory over the disease.

Through her mother's courageous and positive attitude, Jing Jjng learned to overcome distress through faith and hope, as well as external support like counseling and other social resources. Eventually, the family was able to overcome difficulties. This was a positive and proactive attitude towards life.

Jing Jing experienced difficulties with her mother together times when there was mixed feelings of grief and joy, and times when there was fears and lost.  However, in the end she could paint a smiling face on the sand.  This was her interpretation of the new life and hope.

# 面具 Mask

我是一個戴著面具的人，你可能覺得我虛偽。
其實你亦可能戴著面具而不自覺，我有幸發現自己的面具。
雖然我仍未拿開面具對人，但內心的感覺比以前踏實。
希望有一日，我有勇氣、有能力以真面目對人和事。
面具真好，面具保護我！
面具讓我安然與世界接觸。
面具，面具，但你卻令我迷失！
面具令我失去自我
沒有面具，我的日子怎過？
沒有面具，我如何面對別人？
沒有面具，我如何面對自己？
我真的需要面具嗎？
我為何要面具？面具幫助我嗎？
沒有面具，我是誰？
我能除下面具嗎？

I am a person wearing with a mask.  May you say I am not hypocrite.
Perhaps you are the same without awareness.  I am glad that I discovered my mask.
Though I cannot take off my mask now, I feel I am real and hopeful.
I hope I feel safe enough to show you my real self
Mask, Mask. You are so wonderful!  You protect me from being hurt.
You made me feel safe.
Mask, Mask. You made me lost myself.
Without you, mask, how can I live?
How can I face others?
How can I face myself?
Do I really need a mask?
Why do I need a mask?
Does the mask really help me?
Without the mask, who am I?
Can I take my mask off?

## V.   CHINESE TRANSLATION

# 序

2004 年，我完成了 300 多頁關於“道，藝術和終身學習”的論文。這本書的誕生是我博士論文的一部分，我也將它與 20 多年的臨床經驗結合在一起。 與大多數創作過程一樣，治療過程是混亂的，甚至醜陋的。 藝術療法將我們的內外世界，幻想和現實聯繫起來。 在這裡，最重要的問題是我們的“忠誠”。從忠誠中，湧現出愛，以便我們能夠痊癒。 只有美麗心靈，才能讓人發掘到人性醜陋的美。 只有擁有同理心，才能觸及人的尊嚴和正直。 只有充滿希望和信任的心靈，才能將幻想變為現實。 只有空靈，才能從無到有，創造一些東西並擁抱悖論。

# 中西文化滙合
# 道德經藝術心理學

道的天性參與每一件事與物

人不僅只是身體,還有精神,理智和感覺

人類有獨特的能力，超越我們的局限性

# 第一部分
# 更新轉化日誌

更新是關于變化，有不同的層次和方向的變化。改變取決于對自我、他人的和世界的看法。 一次我在奧黑爾機場，看見一個大廣告牌， 上面寫著，" 只要按下一個按鈕，它可以更新你的生活。" 更新就是這麼簡單嗎？ 在外面的世界是那麼容易！在我們的內在世界是那麼容易嗎？

一個有抑郁症和強迫症的當事人坐在我辦公室裏。 她說," 我癱瘓在電腦前。我討厭自己，因爲我討厭我的父母，我想要復仇 ......" 我真誠地希望能有一個按鈕可以立刻改變更新了她的生活。 我們可以按一下按鈕，改變外面的世界，但我們不能改變我們的內心世界。

老子道德經哲學尋求默觀自然，及根藉西方基督教文化的更新變化過程的藝術。兩者最終目的和成果是達到天（神）人合一的精神狀態。這終極的內在自我認同經驗，縱是外面世界的變化，也不能輕易動搖的。

# 1. 矛盾‥意識的學習

天下皆知美之爲美，斯惡矣。皆知善之爲善，斯不善矣。故有無相生， 難易相成，長短相形，高下相傾，音聲相和，前後相隨。恒也。是以聖人處無爲之事，行不言之教；萬物作而弗始，生而弗有，爲而弗恃，功成而不居。夫唯弗居，是以不去。

陰和陽的關系建立穿越宇宙，大和小，男性和女性，之間的張力。道的根基在于對立的原則，但並不排斥對方：積極與消極或北方和南方的都是在同一個系統，只是在系統中的異同不同方面。 陰和陽之間的關系意味著"相互產生"。它反映了所有事物的不可分割的相互關聯性。每一個動作都有其互補的作用。

陰和陽的原則不是西方人稱之爲 "二元論"，但相當明確的二元性表達一個隱式的統一體系。 它們就像不同，但分不開的一枚硬幣，或脈沖和時間間隔在振動。卻沒有一個最終的可能性，幸運和不幸，生和死，無論是在規模較小或致大，來和去永遠沒有開始或結束 。

陰和陽的原則，道往往被假設是相對性的價值。然而，超越對立是道！道是絕對的。道德經，實際上是 "超越贊美之歌，一切整體性和絕對的道 (Maurer, 1985) 。" 道，一種轉身逃避的相對價值使我們能夠完成道中的整體性，而不采取勝負。

# 2. 在矛盾裏選擇，開展精神之旅

第三十三章

知人者智，自知者明。勝人者有力，自勝者強。知足者富。
強行者有志。不失其所者久。死而不亡者壽。

人類有一種內在的衝動，渴望自由和平衡 (和諧) 是人的天性，重拾及其對原始統一性的關系。 成熟的內在生命是人類表明 "對自然的恒定" 的法規，也不斷恢複平衡的努力。在個別的歷史，在世界歷史上，驅動展開走向統一與平衡是自然的人性。我們不能消除的事實： 是無可能生活在一個完全健康的世界，但我們可以做出意識的選擇。學習在矛盾中選擇是自我經歷成長的確認："存在于昨日的的矛盾方式加劇，經理解成爲末來的行爲價值" (Freire, 1973)。在經典的漢語中，道的整體性僅僅是指 "道"，即在之前和之後發生的事情之間有一個聯系 (Clarke, 2000; Cooper, 1981)。在道的陰和陽對立之間有意識選擇是 "動態聯盟的合一" (The unity of life in dynamic flux)。

尋找 "自我" 是一種一步一步的成長經驗。自我是一個過程，包括時間的使用，智力，情感，經驗，和如何重整存放在有意識的和無意識領域的圖片，我們的個人歷史博物館。這個想法是有意識地發生了什麼。 個人達到不同程度的認識和知識，極具個人化。 這一過程既痛苦又有益。 創造一個新的畫面，經曆自我意識，作爲過去和現在，一起來創造一個整體，可能意味著一部分勝過其他部分的構成。這裏的道是指"自我認識和自我約束是主要的成績 ...... 其結果是洞察力‥感知特定社會現象背後中較大的影響的能力" (Maurer, 1985)。過程中非常重要的是個人學會談判的意義、 目的和價值，批判思維、 反思理性而不是被動地接受；我們可選擇心靈平衡的潛力。

# 3. 道的本質:人的尊嚴

第三十四章

大道泛兮，其可左右。萬物恃之以生而不辭，功成而不有。衣養萬物而不爲主，可名于小；萬物歸焉而不爲主，可名爲大。以其終不自爲大，故能成其大。

每一件事情有其特殊的性質，而來自一個道，合一所有。道的天性是內在的精神，我們可以體驗基本統一。 所有的東西依賴于它的生命，道也不拒絕他們 (Murray,1959 )。 道是廣闊和統一的整體，包括所有的觀點和所有的現實，給所有現實同等價值。我們叫它們以不同的名稱，在他們的起源都是同一個。這種等同性是一個謎中之謎。(It is the gate of all wonder)。

道，產生萬物，滋養它們、開發它們、促進他們 ；完善他們，使他們成熟，撕裂他們也保護他們。 我們真正的自我來自一個事實，他或她是沒有區別: "所以聖人不遵循這種區分，在天堂是照亮所有" (Murray,1959 )。 真正的自我是超越區別、 概念和標簽。

看其無數的形式，我們可以看出在生活的規律，到處都有深層渴望轉變衝動。 每一個人的內在生命在于更新變化，進入一種更豐富和更深層次的存在狀態，這種期望是無法抗拒的衝動。轉型的衝動源于要沖破局限與不足的願望，這是人類珍貴的自由意識。這也是內在生命 (真我) 從家庭，社會制度給予的角色及標簽 (假我) 的蛻變過程。一個人感受到迷失與痛苦，只因爲無知的被 "假我" ，虛假的人生本質主導生命 (Maurer,1985) 。 Maurer 反映人尋求試圖控制現實而給予命名。 這不是老子的教導。

第三十二章

道常無名樸。雖小，天下莫能臣。侯王若能守之，萬物將自賓。天地相合，以降甘露，民莫之令而自均。始制有名，名亦既有，夫亦將知止，知止可以不殆。譬道之在天下，猶川谷之于江海。

霸權主義，命名和標記是在人們心中，螺絲著阻礙看到連接。 現代知識支離破碎：人不以一個人爲定義。卻按性別、 顏色、 性取向。。。等區分。 是的，我們需要爲了學習而學習命名。 一旦學會了，我們需要忘掉它，小心的使用主觀刻板的標簽定義人類。從限制和社會化的自我，從社會標簽和外部期望的公約，道追求內在生命的自由。然而這並不意味著道放棄或離開世界。道，不能立法或制度化。它與自由的西方個人主義的權利是非常不同 。 道提醒我們致力于自由和個人的尊嚴，而不接受形式的個人主義。人類不僅是身體，而且也有理性，感覺，精神和獨特的能力，超越我們的局限性 (Clark,2000 年)。 老子認爲，仿效道的行爲會帶來個人，最可能接近內在的和諧生活，與實際地實現人生的真谛。


# 4. 接納改變:危機即轉機

第二十五章

有物混成，先天地生。寂兮寥兮，獨立而不改，周行而不殆，可以爲 地母。吾不知其名，強字之曰道，強爲之名曰大。大曰逝，逝曰遠,遠曰反。故道大，天大，地大，人亦大。域中有四大，而人居其一焉。

人法地，地法天，天法道，道法自然，道是一種動態變化 。我們的生命是變動的！事實上，你身體的活著是有不斷的新層代謝的變化。在我們的物質世界從破壞中建立是常見的，麥子必須枯萎，植物再可以出現，當四季轉移，萬象更新。但當談論生活的變動，我們都害怕改變。因它奪去了我們的安全感，我們已經習慣的地方，人物，情感。這是我們的困境：就像地球繼續轉，變化亦會來。 總是會在不同形式或在危機中損失。危機像個大馬力的聚光燈迫使我們去關注我們的生活，自己和我們的關系。重點是你在一個人生階段。 就在這些時刻，你是主角的給予機會自我反省與靈性的啓示，我們真正的自我誕生。當我們面對危機或創傷時的痛苦是如此之大，使我們的情感已麻痹了。此刻，我們被迫感受一切，它迫使你進軍的勇氣。你並不知道你原來擁有的儲備——信念、希 望和愛是那麼豐富。

中國成語說：“乘風破浪”。如沖浪手學習沖浪，我們朝著當前正在跨越的邊緣，順勢是最好的方法。我發現處理痛苦和危機：要深入它而不臣服于我們的痛苦，也不是抗拒。與我們的痛苦一起跳舞，而不是遠離它。 學習與我們的痛苦跳舞意味著不避免不安或害怕，我們有意識地探索感情而選擇它。它意味著談論我們甯願忘記的東西。它意味著我們 的時間和空間，心裡問：沈溺于悲傷的行爲是否唯一出路？田恩如此的 描述:

> “痛苦是如此強烈，它讓我窒息而死的感覺。這幾天我並肩戰鬥壓倒性的痛苦和恐怖的感覺。 我獨自一人，疼得難以忍受。 我開始繪制一系列心畫。我開始意識到我的傷口，傷害了我這麼多的最深處。癱瘓，我總是想要逃跑，它卻傷害更大。這一個晚上，在繪圖桌旁坐下來，我被沈默包圍著。我對我發生的痛楚停止了抵抗，像奇跡出現了 ...”

## 5. 無爲:學習放手

道有虛空作它的起源，但它的功能只有通過虛空動態存在。這裡是指排空自己或自己謙卑的 (Maurer, 1985)。 虛空是關乎豐滿 (Cheng, 1994 ; Richards, 1989)。 事實上，它是使一切都充分實現他們完整的豐滿的虛空。 因此可以說， "道是一個空的容器；這就是它的有用性。 老子以具體的實例演示虛空的用途‥"
第十一章

三十輻，共一轂，當其無，有車之用。埏埴以爲器，當其無,有器之用。 鑿戶牖以爲室，當其無，有室之用。故有之以爲利，無之以爲用。

通過虛空，心，能成爲本身和整個世界的模型或鏡子；心靈可以擺脫偏見和成見。在處理虛空和被認同的原始的虛空，道，人類發現自己作爲 "主體"。他 / 她能掌握空間和時間的節奏，和律法的變革。

第二十二章

曲則全，枉則直，窪則盈，敝則新，少則多，多則惑。是以聖人抱一爲 天下式。不自見，故明；不自是，故彰；不自伐，故有功；不自矜，故 長。夫唯不爭，故天下莫能與之爭。古之所謂「曲則全」者，豈虛言哉！ 誠全而歸之。

痛苦可以幫助我們成長，發現隱藏的寶藏，知道存在于我們的精神財富。 從生至死，生活是一系列的痛苦，但在另一邊是新的開始；學習放手過去，擁抱明天。當然，我們將與喜悅共存悲傷，轉化更生危機和逆境。 田恩繼續畫她受傷的心。 她解釋說， "我開始明白虛空心靈的意思。 我不知道我需要首先經曆痛苦的考驗。 它是痛苦 ......"

虛空也鏈接到"無"。 無意味著非存在的現象，但不意味著非現實 。 "無爲手段" 概念是，負克制生活，但向前邁進，並伸出手去超越現實的道。 什都不做卻是種方式完成的事情；結果從是做事的唯一途徑。 (Maurer,1985) 無爲動不做，但需要培養參與心內靜止的方式而獲洞悉事件的發生。不是 ... 自由的不做什麼，障礙就會消失。是靜觀其變。 無爲，被動等待某事發生，卻變成了一種積極的力量。通過簡單的意識方式，由那些事情自然發生。它是洞察力，容忍生活的困惑，直到問題的答案表面出來。

## 6. 悟我是誰 ？

通過在衝突中有意識的學習，我們尋求實現我們在社會中的位置有相當大的進展。 我們作爲 "主體" 人類有能力感知在特定的社會現象背後的影響。 這個發現的過程是 "悟" 實現認知 (Realization) "我是誰？" Who am I? 在漢字中的實現 "悟" 意味著心到達完全的理解。 它從五種感官，象征著所有的事情和完成。 數字 "5" 代表五種感官‥五行、 五 色、 五味和五個系統的身體。 當心與五個感官是在和諧的知悉。 這將導

致 "悟" 。

我們的感情來自五種感官：眼睛看(色)，耳朵聽(聲)，嘴裏嘗嘗(香)，鼻聞(味)，身體觸碰(觸)。 感情告訴我們該做什麼，但我們知道該怎麼辦之前，首先需要知道我們的情緒。 一切是 "情緒" (Emotion) 這個詞開展我們的生活。

> 我看到水仙花從土壤出來，她穿著一件黃色的裙子，在風中跳舞，吹在我臉上，是一個溫柔的觸摸。我聞到草香；它是新鮮和甜蜜，我躺在綠色的草地上，想像我睡在雲上，自由和快樂。到了晚上，我躺在我的床上，聽著雨點落打聲，節奏跳動我的心靈。 我在品味春天的人生。

當我們醒來張開眼睛時，無論你想要看或不想看，我們都被圖像轟擊著。 這些圖像滑行通過你的頭腦，而且對你的心靈說它們的話。 這些圖像移動通過你的想法，龐大權力去影響你的感覺與行動。如果我們沒有過濾汲取這些訊息，那就成爲你的思維導向。我們必須找到感受的能力，它是體驗（Experiencing）生活的第一步。 體驗生活是通往警覺 (Consciousing) 悟 "我是誰？" 的必然條件。 "自我發現"(Self discovery) 的旅程，是在天與地之間找到你的位置。

道是無限的，但並沒有提供有發掘自我詳細的信息。現代心理學理論填補和豐富我們理解自我的形成。 Erickson (1982 ) 的 "人類發展的八個階段" 應對陰與陽的理論原則。根據該原則，成長是一個終身的過 程。在每個階段，我們要面對危機和變化之間的選擇。 解決由內在和外在衝突的八個階段，我們身心獲得平均發展和能掌握八個基本美德：信任感，意志力，奮進力，能幹，忠誠心，愛心，關愛心，滿足，才能把握豐盛人生。通過在每個階段的轉型，達到一種可能精神的整體性、 完整性和智慧 ：真實的自 我實現，正如道說：

> 道生萬物，其美德滋養他們，每個人按其性質形成，每一個完善根據其強度 ......
> 他根據道，行事的人成爲一個道同。 他踏實的美德成爲一種美德。( Wing, 1986)

發掘自我要求我問自己困難的問題‥我是誰？你是誰？我活著是人？ 我的人生怎樣交功課？幸福是什麼？ 什麼是痛苦嗎？ 這些問題都將帶你一個新的解放。你重生過程中的縮影。 提問和回答這些問題需要很的大勇氣和消化內在的情緒。它意味著看到你自己的部分，你已經遺忘或否認的。 出生絕非易事，考慮母親懷胎九個月及分娩過程的痛苦。 當父母握著這新的生命時，痛苦變成歡樂和慶祝的生活。 所以，如果你是在分娩自我的過程中，知道這是你生活的強大而神聖的時刻。你在這旅程，無論怎樣，不要試圖轉身回走其他的路。無處可去，只有向前。 最好的辦法是去跨越它。

沖浪到水深之處，我們要在黑暗中尋找光明。這並不容易，但得來的平安非文字盡描述。一個人踏上內在生命的旅程，將會發現所有被覆蓋在潛意識 (Subconscious) 中的內心沖突，被壓抑的記憶、 得不到滿足的潛能，隱藏的恐懼。。。 現在隱藏的一切將由明燈，道的光明清洗淨和愈合。這是內在的心靈醫冶和更生變化。

# 7. 道與更新變化

幾乎每個人在一生中，至少一次醒來,幾乎每個人都可以迅速又睡著 了。 但通過他們瞌睡的日子，他們還是隱約記得，那個時候的覺醒開悟。 一個當事人寫道‥

　　漆黑的夜晚
　　我的心彙
　　我在天空尋找著你
　　深暗的天空
　　孤獨

　　神啊!
　　你在哪裏?
　　你的承諾在哪裏?
　　與我的悲傷和憂慮
　　我可以和誰說話?

　　安靜孤獨停息，心悴耐心等待
　　突然，閃爍的光出現在天空的盡頭
　　它是一顆璀璨之星
　　哦,是你閃爍的燈
　　不是明亮的太陽
　　但是,你還在這裏！

中國哲學使用部分整體對比，而不是一多對比： "要捕捉道作爲現象，就必須區分什麼有限的東西，是不能測量無限" (Ames, 1983)。 道，事情就是的那樣，是零件的所有道的總和。 Cleary (1987) 認爲這是 "生命本質科學之科學" 。 經歷一個人的完美結合，天（神）人合一的狀態是道的最終目的和成果。當外在和內在一體化實現，我們發現自己在不朽的境界被保護著。在天與地之間，確立其健康的身份和定位。那是達到自我肯定的 "神秘経験" (Clarke, 2000)。尋求天（神）人合一的和諧境界，道可稱 爲一種自然神秘主義 (Rowely, 1959)。 根據 Chang (1963)， "理解 "道"，作爲一種內心的體驗，我們必須區分主體與客體之間就消失了。它是直觀的、 直接的認識，而不是導引、推理邏輯分析或智力的過程" 。 以下一詩人寫:

　　風聲索索，竹橫影蔓，流水淙淙，在虛谷下要望著神職人員的背景，使我知道自己太心急於每一件事情的結果。我要給自己時間，按著生活程序，按部就班，從簡以雜，一步一步的做下去。日出而作，日入而息。 讓生活持之以恒，勿讓自己紊亂。我在何方？在樹蔭下，物我兩忘，在幽幽的情懷裏!

如禪者，悟，有許多層次的實現。從臨時的經驗到 "頓 悟" ，到 Welwood 描述(1979) 的 "超越自我" 和 "神人合一" 的境界。通過黙觀靈性紀律的生活，我們可以找到我們內在的自我，我們原始的本性。開悟並不意味著只看到自己，卻也同時了解別人的東西；有辨別能力並不意味著只聽到自己，卻也聽其他的東西；滲透只了解自己，也了解其他的事情。打開方式時，我們將在我們的內心找到神。

更新變化過程中的關系。 Welwood (2000 ) 表明更新變化涉及到我們的開悟實現穿透身體，感性和理性的密集的構思，如此一來精神可以完全集成到個人和人際關系，以便個人生活可以變成透明容器，爲終極的真理或神的啓示。

# 第二部分

# 身心靈整合日誌

我一直對更新變化過程甚感興趣，尤其是在藝術創作的範圍內。我最早的童年記憶，是不能忘記父親專注于繪圖時的背影。他總是告訴我，　"在畫像中最重要的事情是 一個人的精神。　妳必須仔細觀察。　每一個人有不同的 內外特點。畫像要捕獲的是 神韻 (神韻是指：思維、　意 識、　洞察力和人類內存所有 五個心理精神狀態，所有的 一切都取決于心 (Maciocia, 1994)。"　我當時太年輕，不能理解我的父親在說什麼。　但當我看著他的畫 （圖1, 2)，它像磁石一樣吸引了我去尋找神韻，人的內在精神狀態。　這種吸引力，不是因爲 他的畫很有名；是我的父親試圖通過繪畫，發送他的訊息，我試著去理解它。

## 1. 藝術作爲與自我的關系

我總是很興奮的觀察藝術家完成繪圖後的面部表情和手勢，他們向世界宣佈："我這位藝術家，在這裏，和我有話要說。 在這裏！是的， 這就是我！"圖紙、 繪畫、 雕刻、交響樂、 詩歌、 舞蹈和戲劇不是簡單的活動。 每一筆，每個輪廓，每個諧音，每行內韻；所有的舞步都是生活，現實片斷的快照。

當一個作品在我的面前時，我先試從我的心靈傾聽。 一個微妙的沈默！我聽到的是畫筆油畫顏料在畫布上的聲音。 隨著聲音響亮和生動，我意會著一句話或兩句，或許一聲尖叫或一聲歎息，也許一笑。 盡管我試著感受畫者的心情，表達的情感。但藝術家的思想很少通過藝術第一次投射給任何觀衆。與此相反，藝術家第一次的思想從自己裏面孕育著。 它是一個表達從自我到自我 。 很多時候，在我提問之前，藝術家難以解釋他們的思維感情。沒有什麼可以理解，直到它表示在藝術作品上，藝術家往往驚訝的是自己的情懷。

作爲藝術家在空白紙上繪制的第一筆，圖像開始其旅程從內的到外。當藝術家添加線條和形狀，圖像一步步成形。藝術家的情感、 想象、 思維、 以及冲突與形成的圖像之間有流動與恒定的作用。 創造過程：孵化 期 (Paving the Way)，啓發期(Incubation)，光照期(Illumination)， 印証期(Verification) 往往是感人至深，充滿了無法形容的描述。只有藝術家可以充分體驗發生的深度。

藝術作品與自我的關系是，藝術作爲自我表達的環境是主觀反應。 每個藝術創作，藝術家描繪了他們的感受，他 / 她的智能，人格發展、 感性敏感、 情感表達、 創造性地參與、 社會性的發展，審美意識也是表達在裏面。


## 2. 藝術作爲與他人的關系

如果藝術創造是自我的關系。那麼，藝術創作是一種自我表達的行爲。 如果我們將藝術定義爲自我表達行爲。那麼，我們不得不問關于自我 (Self) 需要得到什麼的機會，才能表達。自我心理學 (Self Psychology) 用不同的理論解釋自我。有一假設，語言(Language)，無論是口頭還是書面，有被困擾的規則和約束，使表達力被抑制而不是釋放 。 但是視覺藝術的實踐不受規則。因此，個人的感覺能比較開放自由的表達出來。在文明限制的生活中，自我表達需要能在建設行爲的藝術創作中履行。我們的日常生活經驗有不同的挫折，積累被壓抑的能量。爲了彼此和諧共處，我們壓抑我們本能欲望，這種鎮壓導致張力。那麼，藝術的活動在緊張的社會上是可被接受和構成個人出路的正能量。 同時，通過藝術創建，個人解決了他 / 她的問題，還客觀上制作，令人滿意和有審美價值的東西。 藝術是一種自我表達，但自我表達不會出現在真空上的。表達對象向外，向著聆聽的人。 那藝術表現形式不僅是自我表達，也是與人另一種交流的欲望。最重要的是，自我表達渴望與溝通的人，在過程中通過更改或要求；在與他人交流形式上完成自我表達。

## 3. 藝術作爲與道的精神之旅

通過道的宇宙原則：單一大膽的假設，中國專注于一個權力滲透整個宇宙 的概念。道的概念 "一" 讓中國藝術家搜索平衡與和諧的經驗。 達到天（神）人合一的精神狀態是終極的藝術成就 。在我創作過程的經驗，很多時我不知怎麼畫，直到幾乎快要完成的作品時才知道。 甚至當我要繪畫特定主題，我仍然，在深層意義上也不知道爲什麼我選擇了某一特定主題，或我如何執行內在自我的工作。當過程發生後，就會出現澄清的情感和想法。 雖然我有一些概念畫什麼，但我寧可不去想太多而繪畫畫面，允許不經意來發現線條、 形狀和形式在呈現它自己的方式。這意外驚喜的空間和畫面使我心裏雀躍。 從這裏，藝術家與創作品有了相互溝通的關系。

我觀察事物或人，不只在表面上，但內在的精神 "氣" 類似于 Kandansiky (1982) 理念的 "內在的聲音" (Inner voice) 。 這些經歷，我發現在我的心裏産生創意的過程是有一個輪子。 此輪包括：

a) 深刻的觀察：我觀察我的精神和靈魂。 在某一個時刻，我可能會迷失在其中。

b) 合理的個性化： 我知道的東西並不等于我理解它。 我明白有些事情不是我生命必需的。 當我看著時鍾時，它不僅僅是一段時間或日期。我把 自己放進去，從那裏出現重要的訊息，我聽到 "ta tec" 聲，也聽到我的心跳聲。 它推著我了解更深層次的意義：我的生存就是用這些長短的針計算。 我甚至可以通過這個時鍾看到生活和死亡。 然後我可以理解死亡，並不是只有當你回到塵土的時間。 我出生時，死亡成爲了連接到我的時間和空間之間的生活。

c) 強烈的感情： 源于我的深刻的觀察和理性的個性化。 只有我有這強烈的感情，只有我可以把它做成我的作品。 強烈的感情是我創造的潛力。

d) 轉型： 是壓縮機的創作過程。 它使我強烈的感情，將轉化爲一個理想 的世界。我可以想象一下飛的天鵝，在森林裏樹木變成舞者的手勢 ...... 它 是轉變的力量。

e) 昇華： 我可以將我的現實與理想，無限的感情與永恒升華合結一致。

## 4. 藝術心理分析治療

藝術與心理治療是我們內心和外面世界，幻想和現實的橋梁。 在這裏， 最重要的問題是 "誠信爲本"。 誠信爲本，從愛出發，便可以治愈心 靈。藝術有怡情養性作用，也有治療 (Healing) 的功效 (Naumbury, Kramer, 1955)。藝術可以直接表達人內心的世界，在繪畫的過程中，藝 術治療師 (Art Therapist) 從旁引導的式指引當事人把情緒表達在話之中，再由當事人解釋敘述畫像 (Images)；同時和術治療師進行對話分析。由此，被壓抑的情緒獲得釋放，混亂的思維得到方向。如此一來， 藝術創作過程遂成爲心靈治療的渠道。藝術能夠靜化人心靈，讓人在安靜中整理混亂的思潮。現代城市化的生活，人與人之間缺乏信任，藝術 治療可成爲抒發情緒的最安全媒體。同時藝術也可以提供輕鬆的環境和氣氛，促進紓解當事人的思想。

根據美國藝術治療協會，富有表現力的藝術治療網絡: 藝術 (音樂、 藝術、 戲劇和等)是心理評估和治療的有力工具。 這就 像心內直視手術: 藝術是我們內在和外在存在的橋，連接到我們的潛意 識 (精神、 智力和情感和行爲)。它還：

- 可以提供客戶一個非威脅途徑涉及到治療過程中。
- 可以鬆開剛度和鼓勵適齡的冒險行爲。
- 可以允許和通過藝術提供客戶發泄，發表( 問題的 ) 公開討論; 訴諸輿論。
- 可以幫助解鎖經驗和促進愈合痛苦的問題。
- 可以繞過口頭的操縱，並更快地明白問題的根源。
- 可以面對和減少否認，通過提供一種真實的記錄的感受和想法。
- 可以幫助解決問題，決策和提高技藝的判斷能力。

臨床心理治師需要盡可能密切觀察方式，在每個人和他 / 她的工作之前。 在聽音樂或畫一幅畫時，客戶可能重新體驗創傷的過去。受過訓練的專業人士都知道爲什麼？怎樣執行或不執行這一進程？而最重要的部分 是支持傳釋痛苦的問題和傷口的愈合。不然，當事人會再一度受創傷。

| 藝術治療是 | 藝術治療不是 |
| --- | --- |
| 1. 心理分析治療 | 手相術 |
| 2. 評估與治療 | 繪繪畫 |
| 3. 了解 | 判斷標籤 |
| 4. 著重過程 | 著重產品結果 |
| 5. 發掘創造力 | 藝術才華 |
| 6. 問題解決 | 藥物學 |
| 7. 建設性處理情緒 | 魔術按紐 |

藝術治療師不能消除痛苦，但可以把痛苦變成祝福。心靈治癒是最有創意的過程，像藝術作品末成形前，藝術家都曾面對混亂，令人困惑的和甚至醜陋的局面。 只有一份美的心靈，才可以從醜陋裡看到美麗。 只有 一顆慈悲的心，才可以觸摸人的尊嚴和完整性。 只有希望和信任，才可以將幻想變成現實。 只有虛空的精神，才能擁抱矛盾，永恒，能從無到有。

# 5. 藝術治療現象學  Phenomenology of Healing in Art

讓我們從現象學角度去分析創造力與藝術的關系。

1955 年 2 月 7 日

我拿起一支粉紅色的粉筆，開始繪畫。我將粉筆橫放在紙板上。因此，繪畫的畫面比較寬敞。我畫了一條弧線，我問自己這是什麼？

> *"思潮在腦海中閃過。。。我覺得我很難接觸到我的內心的感受，一些東西阻礙著我的情緒。"*

我拿起一支黑色粉筆，畫了一條直線在粉紅線上,這形成了一只眼的形狀，挂在紙的邊緣。

> *"那條黑線使我注意到我對自己的大學生活很有挫敗感。我不感到書本的學習能貫徹在我的生命中，失去了一些東西。也許是我的文化，或許是我的情感。我不知道如何表達內心的感受。有時，我想拒絕學習。"*

我拿起黃色粉筆,將那眼狀圖案填滿。

> *"我需要一些光彩和一些令我鼓舞的東西。"*

之後，我在眼狀圖案周圍加上紅色,綠色。我將空白填上橙色和紫色。 那形狀擴展，我再用淺藍色和黃色加上陰影。這個抽象的形狀轉移後成 一個像變了型的人體
> *"當那形狀擴展，我想這是我的轉移(Shifting)。我認識到身在外國的環境，我必須學習到能屈能伸，我要適應新的環境，縱使有時我不喜歡。 當時間的流逝，我的自我形象圖畫變了形。"*

鈴聲電話響起了，我在加拿大的妹妹打電話給我。當我跟他談話時，我拿起鉛筆繼續繪畫，加上陰影，加深邊緣線，那形狀就顯明出來。

> *"哦！原來我沒有理會自己的內心感受，我差不多麻木了。"*

那變形的人體完成，但仍不斷的改變 （圖 3).

> *"也許我也在改變，在中西文化的沖突之下，我的生命也在改變。"*

**在創造活動中,我經驗到藝術作品的産生是透過——**

1. 我的意志活動我嘗試表達和接觸我的内心心靈活動: 視覺影像，渴求，觀念，意義和感受。這些被隱藏的知覺從制造藝術品的過程中能得以顯明出來。

2. 我的體力創作活動中—— 調配顏色；移動畫筆從一空間到另一個空間;扭做黏土；停頓；靜思；坐姿；凝視——我嘗試將外在特別在的物象 (External objects) 融會於我内心的心靈活動中。

3. 舒暢和自由的環境中逐漸地，我驚豔到生命的轉化(Transform)：讓自己醒覺地釋放那些内心意念——一些理想中的形象，一些固有定格的概念，期望表現的效果， 想像想到別人怎樣判斷我的繪畫——對于這些内心的意念我在不介意和 在乎。

4. 開放地接受自己我的感覺經驗逐漸增加。我經驗到自己的存在。透過創作活動 , 借著顏色，物料，我經驗到内心的心靈世界和外在世界愈來愈融在一起，感到 一個整全。有時，我沒有計劃的把顏色放在畫紙上。我卻會醒覺地知道這是代表什麼？這種醒覺是超過我的理性，這樣的過程使我了解發生什麼事。

5. 藝術創作成爲爲一項對我生命有意義的。這過程——

 a)對話溝通(Dialectic) 例如：我拿起床黃色粉筆,將那眼狀圖案填滿。

  *"我需要一些光彩和一些令我鼓舞的東西。"*

 b)彼此溝通 (Interactive) 例如：那形狀擴展,我再用淺藍色和黃色加上陰影。這個抽象的形狀轉 移後成一個像變了型的人體。

  *"當那形狀擴展，我想這是我的轉移(Shifting)。我認識到身在外國的環境，我必須學習到能屈能伸，我要適應新的環境，縱使有時我不喜歡。當時間的流逝，我的自我形象圖畫變了形。"*

 c)聯系溝通 (Synergistic) 例如：

  *"也許我也在改變，在中西文化的沖突之下，我的生命也在改變。"*


（圖 4～15 是25年前繪畫的，這裏顯示從藝術經歷自我更新變化過程。）

# 6. 與心像藝術國畫名師張恆先生討論藝術心理

2017 年 8 月

劉：　從兒童美術老師到藝術治療師，那幾本書改變我的事業人生。很高興今天能夠老師討論心理學藝術。你是心像主義國畫藝術創始人。可以談是怎樣的由來？

張：　心像是我創作的泉源，因為心是靈活思想，左右感情的原動力。心像是一種精神的變化，有改變循環作用，可以凝聚或分散，離合思想產生無數的行為。心像綜合著理性與感性，把大自然之美與內在生命的永恆結合在一起，能擴充想像空間，把知性和激情不斷交替，促進藝術的發展。

劉：　很高興心像主義能概括一個人的理性，感性，行為與精神的狀態。 而不是很多現代哲學思維的片段，或單一學說的偏重。最近在列治文市府大廳展出長 252 米《感悟洛磯情》 山水畫卷其中的部分片段。動機是從何而來？

張：　自 26 年前從台灣移居加拿大以來，就被北美的自然山水所打動，並深深地愛上這片土地。每年都多次駕車去洛磯山脈寫生，以美麗山水風光為創作背景，樂在其中。 為了創作這幅山水畫卷，前後醞釀了26 年, 並花了整整 6 年時間來完成，「我從卑詩大學 (UBC) 人類學博物館開始畫，然後一路前行，經過史丹利公園 (Stanley Park)、卡比蘭奴吊橋 (Capilano Suspension Bridge)、內陸賀普 (Hope) 鎮，一直沿著洛磯山脈東行至班芙國家公園 (Banff National Park), 再到賈斯珀國家公園 (Jasper National Park), 繞了一圈，直至回到鄰近 UBC 的家。期間經歷了春夏秋冬四季景觀。」多年積累的數百張畫稿，從中挑選 142 張連接成這幅總長達 252 米的山水長卷，從畫中可以看到洛磯山脈的森林峽谷、像徵原住民文化的圖騰岩畫柱、風景秀麗的高山湖泊以及變化萬千的瀑布冰川。

劉：　聽說還有一些內心的故事引發創作動機，是甚麼呢？

張：　小時候,問父母我從何以來? 他們說我從水邊，石頭中爆出拾回來的。因此，我鐘情於大自然 .....

劉：　這裡藝術對你來說帶來一股積極向上之正能量。但這樣的答案，在我遇見的當事人中，類似你的故事，有可能會變成有精神心理不健康的情況。你能夠解釋藝術給你怎樣的心靈力量？

張：　心可以跨越一切物質與精神的障礙，有曰 '吾心即宇宙,宇宙便是 吾心。" 心能神遊宇宙，無限制，自由，樂觀，進取。所以，重視心像擁抱真情作為創作的中心思想。心像無限，包羅萬像，具像抽像中存在著理想，幻想，夢想，冥想，感想，聯想，推想，回想，這些心像都是藝術創作的起源。

劉：　這裡我對心像的理解，就如 "深度心理學" 的 "Ego Self 自我"，自我不等於中國人理解的自私。自我包含有內在性和外在性的心理成長，所謂知己知彼都需要。不同的年齡階段有不同的心理美德的培育鍛煉。剛剛說到很多不同的思想，有可能會是歪想的，不切實際的，沒有建設性的，怎樣分辨呢? 似乎從藝術角度來說，都是可以接受的思想? 畫壇上就不多人去欣賞，如梵高的畫在生時不被珍惜；死後才被利用為市場價值。在藝術治療師角度來說，每一幅畫是很珍貴，它是人與人之間的溝通橋樑。

張：　心路有兩方面，一是內向，一些外向。因此，心向，在決定畫家的畫路和主張。隨著愛好，理念用心的開發新境界；向內的心路可以探討 "真像"，外向的認識可以獲得更多存在 "假像"。所以畫家的心路兩者都要，讓心像生活在心路間的門裡門外，不能只在閉門造車，也不能只在浪跡天涯，或以怪亂為崇高的至高點。

劉：　在我對創造過程研究中，這裡就是說左右腦功能，感性與理性，現 實與理想，實踐，認知及潛意識的整合。似乎若不能分辨 "真像" 和 "假 像" 兩者之間，就沒有 "心像" 了!

張：　過去傳統，真像，是靈性的探討。藝術家要能深切對待生活，生命的真實，才有好的藝術作品。藝術的真像是道的本體。一般有創作力的藝術家，都為內向心靈真像表達的成份大於外向物質假像描述。雖然現代藝術的發展有，變像，大於真像的趨勢和潮流；心像的存在與發展 是沒有斷層的，其本質自古至今，都是大同小異，在表現上隨著，恆變，是不變的道理在循序漸進。

劉：　可以這樣說嗎！真像是精神形像，心靈的修養；假像是物的形像，外向物質描述。而心像是心物合一與道的本體融合? 道可超越我們身體，思想，情緒，及社會制度的種種局限性。在藝術歷史不同的流派裡，作品都可呈現心像，是乎畫家的靈性修養?

張：　真像多為科學辨證的實相，假像多為主觀誤判的印像、意像。真像是真，假像常彼善與美左右影響，產生與真不同現像。真像是自然現像，假像是人為個體因素產生的現像。中國的藝術發展多為天人合一，物我合一中庸之道發展。

劉：　那麼抽像，超現實派是真像? 物我合一就是心像?

張：　抽像不一定是真像，抽像是具像的另一面，但是常被誤認的抽像的，卻是真像、實像情形也有，例如花蕊、岩石機理的放大。這種的誤解是抽像，是因為不常見 (看不懂是什麼?) 而被例為抽像罷了。所謂現實有形與無形的區分，無形的如精神、思想。超現實有再現物像的意思, 也就接近自然物的真相了。物我合一是心源初心與外相交融，是創作新相的根源之一，所以常言 "像由心生"。即心是因，相是果的因果關係!

劉：　這解答了我思維上一些予盾問題。　這兩年爭扎人性的真像與假問題。　藝術家看到的，科學家末必看得到。現代的科學研究雖有客觀辨証，但多只是片面，以片概全或走極端，變得支離破碎。不包含全面和心的深度，就不能談心物合一了。

張：　原則上真像不變或少數會變，假像是不穩定的，會因人、時、地不 同而改變。

劉：　因為本質上，真善美是永恆的。而相對論就可以魚目混珠！

張：　心物要合一，要應物像形，移情於物。相對論在藝術創作上，有逆向反思維，是好的。

劉：　你是指在繪畫佈局上的表現，一幅畫已有了一個框架，這也像是類比的絕對。在框架範圍中，相對是好的。在心理學裡，在人性真善美的原則下知己知彼的洞察力，也運用相對的理解。　藝術思維的包容性又廣也深! 連瘋瘋的都可以! 那麼現代潮流，意向派，下意識與潛意識是隱藏的；畫家如何把心像呈現？

張：　有了動念才會有意的表達，但本心，初心是還沒有浮現的。意向追求，但慢慢又會發現心魔。人的初心是在人的靈性上 ，經過正正反反面，藝術家必備一把智慧的劍，著重心靈的修養。心靈不被心塵矇蔽才能明心， 不斷探索追求人生的真善美。真是原始性，善是經過社會文化，教育誘導出來的道德準繩。

劉：　所以，你是說一件藝術作品能夠浮現創作者心像的本心，初心是有 生命的。如果有意沒有心的話，那藝術創作就沒有意義和生命感。這種說法就如在藝術冶療過程中，我與當事人透過繪畫將潛意識浮現，共同探索和誘導的方向。如此一來，那作品不論好醜，完成或末完成；都是有生命的藝術品！

張：　我再補充: 1. 內向的體驗和外向的觀察，即，外師造化，內心發源。 說明宇宙本體法則的兩儀一元化。外向認識越深，內向的觀察越強。也是人和自然融合為一的，天人合一之道。2. 超前性認知不止於藝術的層面，要追求更高的哲學意義，在有可限的藝術領域中發展到無限的空間, 所以中國畫藝術要順應時代，又要超越時代。3. 在現與表現合一，理性於非理性的融合，表達作家的精神本質，不違背人性的發揮。4. 離合共 一，把繪畫的四綱包容統一在一起，不做極度的對立或偏廢。

劉：　老師的藝術彰顯生活升華美的崇高和諧自然景界。“天人合一”心到筆到，我也曾在繪畫創作中經歷；但只是一瞬間的領悟，很快又回到現實中。上山還須落山， 我選擇了在藝術的真善美彰顯人類心靈治癒的創意過程。在心靈治療過程中，我與當事人也有剎那間的共湧合一 “吓吓頓悟”境界。 老師的鼓勵激發我再記取我的理念、人生從幻想到現實世界的變化。藝術作品末成形前，藝術家都曾面混亂，令人困惑的和甚至醜陋的局面。 只有一份美的心靈，才可以從醜陋裡看到美麗。 只有一顆慈 悲的心，才可以觸摸人的尊嚴和完整性。只有希望和信任，才可以幻想變成現實。 只有虛空的精神，才能擁抱矛盾，永恆，能從無到有。

張：　是的，用美的心靈看世界！不在乎好壞、美醜…都是心像藝術創作的泉源。心像藝術在表達作者的內心精神世界，詮釋真善美。可以將人的思想靈性和本質內涵，發揚光大。

劉：　這是我寫論文時期的畫作（圖4～15)，大部份都是長宣紙的一半。藝術是不可思議。25年前我並不知自己畫甚麼。現在才悟到對我有更深意義。

張：　人生的歷程像心電圖,是跳動的，不跳動靜止時，生命便結束了。 藝術創作的過程，如果前後不能持續藝術生命也就沒有了。25年前的思維是潛意識的存在，今天顯現事實，是我所謂的藝術生命是必備過去、 現在、未來。這也是我研究生們常提到的一件事。

劉：　可以詮釋過去，現在，未來的理論多一點啊?

張：　過去，現代，末來，真像的突變機率不大；兩極，中庸的思想都不會消失。這就是，心像，能夠決定我們作品走向的原因，也是真像會大 於假像的肯定性。

劉：　啊！怪不得很多當事人都以為我能為他們看相命! 其實，我們有直覺與洞悉心像的本領！我覺得心像藝術與心理治療有很多聯繫性。

張：　現代藝術的發展趨勢，大都是由知覺到直覺，由客觀到主觀，由具像到抽像，由理性到感性，其實都在強調表白自己的情感，思想和直觀感受，這是心像的表白。凡事追求都得從根源去探索，忠誠於自己的心像；用客觀哲理去求證。珍惜個體根性的存在，善用和諧的相對論說和絕對論能和平共處。

劉：　是的 ，毋忘初心!這也正是我十多年前寫的論文："道 , 藝術與精神健康" 所探討的重點。現代哲學思維只取相對而拼棄絕對，因而造成很多心靈的空蕩。我很滿足的在自己的辦公室默默地上作。現在再自己繪畫創作、卻有點習慣，要多與你的心像藝術話 , 應能擴闊藝術領域。我只想讓人理解藝術的真善美 -- 人的致寶!

張：　對藝術的熱忱是走藝術道路的第一條件。把繪畫當修養，人有精進生命才有意義。傳統只要了解，不能走回頭路。在己有的基礎上尋找出 路自由發揮，才沒有壓力。發現未來，自得其樂的心，豐富人生。

劉：　感謝張老師的時間與指導！更抽空為這本書作中文校對及提要。"感悟洛磯情"創世界健力士最長中國山水墨長卷畫,要做的事情還很多。 祝願你身心靈健康，把中國藝術精神文明在西方文化中發揚光大！

# 第三部分
# 終生學習日誌

道是無限的

它提供了我們無限的機會學習和成長

道的經驗是類似于藝術家的創造力

生活是藝術，在其動態變化的合一裏培養生活

# 1. 自我的意義

當我們遇到極端的對比：如醜與美，傷害與愛戀，孤獨與親密 …… 在這些時刻，我們開始看得更遠，感覺在我們的骨髓也要哭出來的 "這是可能的！世界不是完全是這樣的。"。 我們可能會開始尋找更廣泛和更深層次的含義，這裡就分拆成很多不同的宗教或精神方向的生活。 耶穌說：我們在天上的父；佛陀描述道在自然 ；儒家呼喊的天啊 ； 哲學家說人類是一面鏡子，像宏觀的一個縮影。無論是一個訊息或是圖像或一個字，它 傳遞了生的意義。

我相信每個心理鬥爭都是尋找著精神的方向。Erickson (2000 )，"心理治療是一種關系，建立在人類的苦難，試圖通過喚醒 "信仰與共享"。 痛苦的精神問題：如 "我們爲什麼會在這裏？"，" 我是誰?"，"怎麼是這樣的痛苦或幸福？"或 "我們去哪兒？" Jung (1965) 結合道和心理治療的智慧：我們看到亮光來實現平衡天堂和地球之間的生活方式。 他說："如果我們以道作爲意識方法，將分離的合一起來，我們可能已經相當接近概念的心理內容 …… 無疑，這種合一的目的是實現有意識的生命。"

道的價值在于它在更高層次的意識上調和對立的力量 ，它被表達作爲光的 象征， 調和極端 ，以達到平衡和崇尚的生活方式。 絕對價值和相對價值並不矛盾： "…… 爲了達到平衡的生活方式和崇尚的生活方式 , 調和極端是心理治 療法的努力嘗試。 榮格 (Jung, 1965) 發現他在實踐多年的心理治療方法與古代道的明智教學不謀而合。" 他說 ：

> 我在實踐的經驗中， 道德經如向我揭示了一種東方智慧和意想不到的方 法 ... 我的專業經驗告訴我，在我的技術中，我一直無意識地被東方的智慧引領著。(Chang, 1963, p.6)

除了我們的局限，還有很多機會去學習和成長。天地之間，內外世界，理性與心性，理智與情感，持有或放手，有無盡的學習機會。我們的優點通常也是我們的弱點。隨著現代社會的分化和專業化，過度成長的優點也表明那些沒有成長的弱點。 Welwood (1991) 說，"成爲一個人類意味著發現我們充實地學習與生活。 這涉及把我們的真我呈現及有意義的活在當下" (p. 15)。

我們經常發現自己處于進退兩難的境地：我應該怎麼做，當有人生我的氣？我對某人生氣 ，怎麼辦？基本上，我們不要立即下判斷。我們要學習，不要把自己分成好和壞，純潔或不純潔的一面。我們不試圖解決這個問題，而是把這一切的情況喚醒我們進一步的成長。我們可以用不同的情境來治愈自己，鼓勵自己走出歧見。因此，我們可以說，"我不知道我要去哪裏 ，但我在道的路上。" 人生有兩種方式，自由或不自由，是我們每一 刻的選擇。 生活只是一個學習過程，提醒及鼓勵我們每一刻選擇溫柔愛心和善良。 我們的精神活動不只局限于一個特定的區域；否則，它會輕易産生失真。靈性修行和個人成長是生活中不可或缺的一部分。

掌握自我是一項終生的旅程，需要通過童年到晚年的整合及持續的學習。道是一個終生學習的經驗，通過日常的努力。 Grigg (1999) 認爲，"沒有魔法，沒有什麼了不起的事。 技能是通過反思、洞察力和培養直覺而得來的”。道是一個整體的經驗，一種相互交織的行動與無爲 ( 陰陽 ) 和多重性與統一性 ( 發散 / 收斂 )。自由湧現在意識 "Concientization Person" 之內；不是來自政府或社會機構的命令。要求 “平等” 研究和政策。我們必須養成一種成功的態度：“虛空自己” 的偏見、自我中心、自眨、階級和種族中心主義，以填補新的潛能和知識。我們需要通過自我反省、矯正和參與來培養這種 “意識” 。

## 2. 道、藝術、終身學習

道是無限，它開辟了無限的機會學習和成長，也是一種只能通過體驗平衡的現象來實現，崇高的意識整合生活方式 (Wilber, 1999; Clarke, 2000)。 Grigg 認爲 , “人類意識的事業是有意義的。所有的經驗都是一 個脫節的糾結 , 必須組織和融入有意義的模式。”《道德經》的第十章，“擁抱道與合一意識”，引入了許多重要的實踐概念，從生命力與意識的結合開始。談到深度靈活性、 淨化的洞察力，運用理性和直覺意識，自然，純真 , 行事無推定：所有這些都被認爲是道家精神的關鍵要素，是被視爲道精神科學的本質和生命 (Cleary, 1987; Wing, 1986)。

道德經的教學既有理性又是直觀的意識：正如文本所說的，“感知小就是 洞察力”。穩守保持叫做力量 ，一個人能發光是返回到洞察力。 這些說明了人類心智的普通官能如何服從于道的高等心智，而不被貶低或破碎 (Wing, 1986)。 “昇華作用的豐富性”，比喻描述了理想的靈活性和堅定性、純真和賦權的能力；掌握能量和保持克制力的關鍵概念 。

當外在不能混淆你的內心時，發現你的本性是最適合的條件。 人的本性是喜愛和諧，好惡焦慮，當精神主導身體時，身體順⋯服從；當身體主導精神時，精神吃力用竭了。 “回歸自然” (Lau,1992) 認識精神將返回到萬物的根源。 我們看著無形，聽聽無聲，在深層的黑暗中，只有看 到光。在沈默的浩瀚，通過死亡，將是開放和平靜。然後不難洞察先例，見到未來 。注意力轉向心理、 審美，和精神境界，往往被忽視的生活。Grigg (1999) 強調 “... 事實上，道，像禪，不是一種生活的哲學；它是藝術。 像藝術過程本身、 道擁抱生活，所有的內在矛盾，將其轉化成創造性的能量，這種經驗平衡和協調緊張的關系。”

道提示注意心理、 審美，和精神境界。 道的生活，是在對立裡找到定位和合一的生活 ，超越了世俗世界的小問題和社會局限。這是一個終身的學習任務。 終身學習之道側重于開發成功，“ 倒空自己的偏見、 自我中 心、 通過自校正反思和培養參與的意識” 它也是生活的藝術。

生活是藝術，培養情感內在的和平，美的欣賞和體驗生活的本身。導向根源和正能量，超越世界的小問題和社會機構的統一生活。道的經驗是類似于藝術家的創造力和審美鑒賞家。 生活的藝術，培養其動態流量（Dynamic flux， Chang, 1963）。無限虛空的空間，道可以吸收不同世界的心理學和藝術，不同的宗教和許多其他方式 (Chang, 1963)。 心理理論對自我的形成提供了詳細的信息。 道給我們深進的方向和框架。 Chang (1963) 注意到，中國道的哲學教我們真誠追求，以此來提升人的精神活動，心理學解釋如何減輕人類的痛苦和達到心理平衛。 因此神秘古老東方的智慧，帶給我們不再是一個謎，但是有益于健康、和諧的生活方式。

尋找自我的意義是一個終身學習的過程。 從對靈性的心理，培養情感內心的平靜的生活之道，自我的中心作用是能夠把事件成爲有意義 (Spence 1987)。 雖然存在著無知和痛苦，靈性表明痛苦和死亡都包括在內，並最終超越的更大的整體，保留我們，以及 — — 客觀地 — — 希望我們好。 有時我們經歷是孤立的；但人類的經驗分享，從上到下 (向內)，和縱橫 (向外)，我們可以發現，我們的參與在一個大型和有意義的整體。 一個人知道他 / 她在天和地之間的位置，作爲一 個 "共同創作者"，他 / 她擁抱著智慧，穩守岡位致力于變革和轉型的突破。 最後，他 / 她在生活中發現有意義的生命，並傳遞及延續這些經驗。

REFERENCE

Ames, R.  (1983).  The Art of Rulership.  Honolulu: University of Hawaii Press.

Bateson, M. C.  (1989).  Composing a Life.  New York: Atlantic Monthly Press.

Bertman, S.  (1999).  Grief and the Healing Art.  New York: Baywook Publish.

Betensky, M.  (1973).  Self-discovery Through Self-expression: Psychotherapy with
     Children and Adolescents.  Springfield, IL: Charles C. Thomas.

Bi, W.  (1999).  The Classic of the Way and Virtue.  Translated by R. J. Lynn,  New
     York: Columbia University Press.

Blofeld, J.  (1973).  The Secrete and Sublime: Taoist Mysteries and Magic.  London:
     George Allen and Unwin Ltd.

Carlsen, B.  (1988).  Meaning-Making: Therapeutic Processes in Adult Development.
     London: Norton Company.

Chang, Chung-Yuan.  (1975).  Tao: A New Way of Thinking.  New York: Harper
     Colophons Books.

Chang, C. Y.  (1963).  Creativity and Taoism.  New York: Harper and Row Publishers.

Cheng, F.  (1994).  Empty and Full.  Boston: Shambhale.

Clarke, J. J.  (2000).  The Tao of the West .  London: Routledge.

Clarke, J. J.  (1994).  Jung and Eastern Thought.  London: Routledge.

Cleary, T.  (1987).  Understanding Reality.  Honolulu: University of Hawaii Press.

Cleary, T.  (1991).  The Essential Tao.  San Francisco: Haper San Francisco.

Cooper, J.  (1981).  Ying and Yang.  Wellingborough: The Aquarian Press.

Corob, A.  (1987).  Working with Depressed Women.  USA: Gowen Publish Co.

Csikszentmihalyi, M.  (1999).  Religious and Philosophical Aspects of Lao-tzu.  New
     York: State University of New York.

Durfee, H.  & Rodier, D.  (eds.), (1989).  Phenomenology and Beyond: the Self and its
     Language.  Boston: Kluwer Academic Publishers.

Ellenberger, H. F.  (1970).  The Discovery of the Unconscious: The History and
     Evolution Of Dynamic Psychiartry.  London: Allen Lane.

Erikson, E. H.  (1982).  The Life Complete Cycle.  New York: Norton.

Erikson, E. H.  (1980).  Vital Involvement World Age.  New York: Norton.

Farrow, J.  (1984).  Spirituality and self-awareness.  Friends Quarterly, 19(2), 213-323.

Feng, Gia-Fu.  (1972).  Tao Te Ching: Lao Tsz.  New York: Alfred A Knopf Inc.

Freire, P.  (1970a).  Pedagogy of the Oppressed.  New York: Herder & Herder.

Freire, P.  (1973).  Education for Critical Consciousness.  New York: Seaburry Press.

Friedman, M.  (1992).  Religion and Psychology: A Dialogical Approach.  New York:
     Paragon House.

Garai, J. E.  (1979).  New horizons of humanistic approach to experience therapies
     and creativity development.  Art Psychotherapy, 6, 177-183.

Gilliagan, C.  (1982).  In a Different Voice: Psychological Theory and Women
     Development.  Cambridge: Harvard University Press.

Goleman, D; Kaufman, P; Ray, M.  (1992).  The Creative Spirit.  New York: Dutton
     Book.

Griffin, R.  (1996). Eyes on the future: converging images, ideas and instruction. Illinois:
     Chicago, Annual Conference of the International Visual Literacy Association. ERIC# 39147.

Hendricks, G.  & Weinhold, B.  (1982).  Transpersonal Approaches to Counseling and
     Psychotherapy.  Denver, Co: Love Publishing.

Igoa, C. (1999). <u>Language and Psychological Dimensions: The Inner World of the Immigrant Child</u>. U.S.; California (Paper presented at the American Educational Research Association, Montreal April, 1999).

Josseleson, R. (2000). Relationship as a path to integrity, wisdom, and meaning. In Young-Eisendrath, P. (2000). <u>The Psychology of Mature Spirituality</u>. London: Routledge.

Jung, C. G. (1958). <u>Psychology and Religion.</u> London: Routledge and Kegan Paul.

Jung, C. G. (1971). Schiller's ideas on the type problem. In Read, H., Fordham, M., Adler, G. (eds), <u>Psychological Types</u>. Princeton, NJ: Princeton University Press.

Jung, C. G. (1983). <u>Memories, Dreams, Reflections</u>. London: Fontana.

P. (ed.)., (2000). <u>The Psychology of Mature Spirituality</u>. London: Routledge.

Keyes F. M. (1983). <u>Inward Journey Art as Therapy</u>. London: Open Court.

Kramer, E. (1958). <u>Art Therapy in a Children' Community</u>. Illinois: Charles C. Thomas Publishes.

Kramer, E. (1987). Sublimation and art therapy. In Rubin, J. (1987). <u>Approaches to Art Therapy</u>. New York: Brunner.

Knowles, M. S. (1980). <u>Self-Directed Learning</u>. New York: Association Press.

Knowles, M. S. (1980). <u>The Modern Practice of Adult Education</u>. New York: Cambridge Books.

Kramer, E. (1972). <u>Art as Therapy with Children</u>. New York: Schoken Books.

Kramer, E., & Wilson, L. (1979). <u>Childhood and Art Therapy: Notes on Theory and Application</u>. New York: Schocken Books.

Lao-tzu (1989). <u>Tao Te Ching (English) A new Translation Commentary</u>. By Ellen, M. Chen. New York: Paragon House.

Lau, S. O. (1992). <u>Return to the Nature</u>. Unpublished Paper.

Lau, S. O. (1993). <u>Art Therapy and Conscious Learning</u>. Unpublished Paper, Northern Illinois University.

Lau, S. O. (1994). <u>A Case Study of the Art Expression of An Eleven-Year-Old Chinese Boy as an Aid in Adapting to the new Society</u>. Unpublished paper at Northern Illinois University.

Lipsey, R. (1988). <u>An Art of Our Own</u>. Boston: Shambhale.

Lord, J. (1987). <u>No Time for Goodbye</u>. CA.: Pathfinder Publishing.

Maciocia, G. (1994). <u>The Practice of Chinese Medicine</u>. New York: Churchill Livingston.

Masters, K. S., and Bergin, A. E. (1992). Religious orientation and mental health. In J. F. Schumaker (ed.), <u>Religion and Menatl Health</u>. New York: Oxford University Press.

Maurer, H. (1985). <u>The Way of the Ways</u>. New York: Schocken Books.

Moore, Charles A. (1968). <u>Philosophy and Culture East and West</u>. Honolulu: University of Hawaii Press.

Mondrain P. (1988). Quoted in Lipsey, R. (1988). <u>An art of Our Own.</u>

Morgan, E. (1974). <u>Tao The Great Luminant</u>. Taipei: Cheng Wu Publishing Co.

Morris, S. (1971). <u>Grief and How to Live with It</u>. London: Allen & Unwin.

Murray, J. (1959). <u>The Sayings of Lao Tzu</u>. Great Britain: Bulter and Tanner Ltd.

Naumburg, M. (1947). <u>Studies of "Free" Art Expression of Behavior Problem Children and Adolescents as A means of Diagnosis and Therapy</u>. New York:Coolidge Foundation.

Naumburg, M. (1953). <u>Psychoneurotic art: Its Function in Psychotherapy</u>. New York:Grune and Stratton.

Naumburg, M. (1966). <u>Dynamically Oriented Art Therapy</u>. New York: Grume and Stratton.

Nouwen, H. (1972). <u>The Wounded Healer</u>. USA: Doubleday.

Nouwen, H. (1974). <u>Out of Solitude</u>. Ave Maria Press.

Nouwen, H. (1982). <u>Gracias! A Latin American Journal</u>. Maryknoll, New York: Orbis Books.

Richards, M. C. (1989). <u>Centering</u>. New England: Hanover, New Hampshire.

Roger, C. (1980). <u>A Way of Being</u>. Mass.: Houghton-Mifflin. <u>Psychotherapy: Theory and Research</u>. New York: Ronald.

Rowley, G. (1955). <u>Principle of Chinese Painting</u>. New Jersey: Princeton University Press.

Rubin, J.  (1984).  <u>The Art of Art Therapy</u>.  New York: Brunner Inc.

Rubin, J.  (1987).  <u>Approaches to Art Therapy</u>.  New York:  Brybber Inc.

Shapiro, E.  (1994).  <u>Grief as Family Process</u>.  New York: Gulford Press.

Simpkins & Simpkins (1999).  <u>Simple Taoism: A Guide to Living in Balance</u>.  Boston: Tuttle Publishing.

Spence, D.  (1987).  Turning happenings into meanings: The central role of the self.  In
    Young Eisendrath, P.  (1987).  <u>The Book of the Self</u>.  New York: New York
    University Press.

Stanage, S.  (1987).  <u>Adult Education and Phenomenological Research</u>.  Florida: Robert
    E. Krieger Publishing Co. <u>Inquiry in Adult Education</u>.  Northern Illinois University.

Walker, L.  (1979).  <u>The Battered Woman.</u>  Unpublished Paper.

Watts, A.  (1961).  <u>Psychotherapy the East and West</u>.  NY: Vintage Book.

Watts, A.  (1975).  <u>Taoism: Way Beyond Seeing</u>.  Boston: Charles E. Tuttle.

Welch, H.  (1965).  <u>Taoism: The Parting of the Way</u>.  Boston: Beacon Press.

Welwood, J.  (1983).  <u>Awakening the Heart: East /West</u>.  Boston: Shemabala.

Welwood, J.  (1991).  <u>Journey of the Heart</u>.  Haprper Perennial.

Welwood, J.  (2000).  <u>Toward a psychology of Awakening: Buddhism. Psychotherapy,
    And the Path of Personal and Spiritual Transformation</u>.  Boston: Shambhala.

Wilber, K.  (1979).  <u>No Boundary, Eastern & Western Approach to Personal Growth</u>. Los Angeles:
    Centa   Publisher.

Wilber, K.  (1983).  <u>A Sociable God: Towards a New Understanding of Religion</u>.    Boston: MA;
    Shambhala.

Wilber, K.  (2000).  <u>Grace and Grit</u>.  Boston: Shambhala.

Wilson, L.  (1987).   Symbolism and Art Therapy.  In Rubin, J.  (1987).  <u>Approaches to Art Therapy</u>.
    New York: Brunner.

Wing, R. L.  (1986).  <u>The Tao of Power: a translation of Tao Te Ching by Lao Tzu</u>.  Garden City,
    New York: Doubleday

Young, E.  (1997).  <u>Voices of the Heart</u>.  New York: Scholastic Press.

Young-Eisendrath, P.  & Miller, E.  (eds.), (2000).  <u>The Psychology of Mature Spirituality</u>.
    London: Routledge.

# ABOUT THE AUTHOR

## 劉思愛　Sze oi Lau

Sze Oi was born in Hong Kong. She studied charcoal and oil painting from her father. 1987, She finished philosophy study at Holy Spirit College in Hong Kong, and graduated Magna cum laude. In 1992, she received her Bachelor of Fine Arts in Printmaking from Florida International University. Between 1993 and 1996, she studied Museum Art Education and Art Therapy under full scholarship at the Northern Illinois University. During this period, she painted with watercolors and received "The Best New Artist Award" at the DeKalb Art Festival.

In 1997, she moved to Richmond, British Columbia to establish her private practice in Art Psychotherapy. In 2000, she founded the "School of Expressive Arts Therapy" and received her doctoral degree in 2004. In 2010, she organized "Hong Kong Psychology of Art Association", offer art therapy diploma programs in Canada and China. Dr. Lau has 25 years art teaching experiences and extensive clinical work around Mental Health issues: Depression, Phobias, Early Psychosis and addiction; and trauma relates to PTSD, Domestic violence and abuse. She is also specialized in right brain visual learning. She promotes and designs personal therapeutic and educational program for children with special needs: such as Autism, Syndromes, learning Delays & ADHD.

Dr. Lau was a finalist for "Richmond Arts Awards" from 2011 to 2013. Dr. Lau is semi-retired after 25 years as a therapist. She is pursuing again her love for art and endeavours to portray the essence of beauty from the inside out.

## Art Work

1984　The Two Innocent Hearts (Charcoal) *Searching for kindness, beauty and truth through children's expression withing the conflicts of life.*

1990　Tao Art (Ink & Water Colors) *The artist learns to perceive with a desirelessness attitude, and to let the* essence of existence, spirit reveal Himself."

1992　Return to Nature (Print making on Zine plates) *Sze oi notes that "The resolution of the paradox in Modernity is to learn to critically negotiate meaning, purpose, and value within the nature principles."*

1993　Golden Silence (Water Colors) *Pictures of quiet, indulge in the silent, is a mind of escape.*

1994　Four Seasons (Water Colors) *It demonstrated here by the artist's spontaneity and 'pure experience' of harmong with Humanity, Earth and Heaven.*

2016　The Emotional Black Hole (Media prints) *The emotional therapeutic process involve paings, love, fears, tears, angers, I gnorance, brokeness, humor, laughter, wisdom....*

2017　Human Essence ( Textile & Canvas) *Life gives scrapes; she puts them together in a beautiful quilt.*

## Awards

1995　Best New Artist Award, Deklb Art Festival

2011　Richmond Arts Award Finalist

2012　Richmond Arts Award Finalist

2013    Richmond Arts Award Finalist
2016    Richmond Mid-Summer Arts Dream 2^nd prize in Art
2017    Richmond Mid-Summer Arts Dream 1^st prize in Art

劉思愛生於香港。父母養育三兒三女, 她排行第三 。小學畢業後，便要在社會工作幫補家庭生活。青少年時期, 熱愛舞蹈並教授中小學生。她更喜歡閱讀，遊歷，對文化言語都感興趣。受父親劉富華薰陶學習油畫, 素描。並在中文大學校外課程學習中國畫兩年。八零年代, 創辦了香港小画家天地教授兒童。 教學之餘，在香港仔聖靈學院修讀哲學，1987 年獲意大利頒發副學士文憑。1989 年赴美國佛羅里達國際大學主修藝術，1992 年獲藝術學士。後以獎學金進入北伊利諾州立大學攻讀藝術治療碩士, 並任助教職位。1994 年獲博物館教育碩士。 1995 年, 完成藝術治療碩士。 1997 年獲取了教育博士候選人的资格，同年移民加拿大温哥華，成為心理治療師為社區服務，2004 年完成博士學位。

劉博士有二十五年教授藝術與及精神心理分析的臨床經驗，亦專長於右腦視像思維與學習的訓練，於 2000 年在加拿大創立 Dr.Art  School of Expressive Arts Therapy。 2010 在香港組織香港藝術心理會，提供及颁發藝術治療法文憑課程。在香港創立藝術心理學會，推動藝術治療法教育。她深信心理精神病是可以預防的，積極參與醫療援助隊在中國各省的精神病院及山區致力精神心理健康培訓工作。過去為了病人她自己無瑕創作。現以半退休時間整理畫作，寫書及藝術創作。

畫作
1984    **两颗童心 (炭筆)** *透過兒童的纯真表情, 以寫實風格記錄人性在沖突中搜索真善美的范式.*
1990    **道的藝術 (中國水墨)** *以一種 "即興" 和  "纯粹的經驗" 的感觉去創作。以 "忘我" 的心態，讓靈光  參與創作其中。*
1992    **回歸自然 (銅版彫印)** *版畫以抽象元素,線條，造型，光線。。。刻畫出後現代主義對人性造成的沖突  與挣扎。*
1993    **静的考驗 (水彩畫)** *在水與色彩的幻化中，不經意地去發現尋找。一点一滴，一絲一扣，留下生活痕跡。*
1994    **四季 (水彩)** *以色彩顯示天、人、地的和谐經驗。當季節來了又走，所有的東西死亡又重生*
2016    **情绪黑洞 （电腦媒体）** *誠信為本，從愛出發生，便可以治愈心靈。*
2017    **人類本质 （碎布補縫藝術油畫）** *生活给了我們擦伤，以藝術靈光她把它併在一起，成為一幅美麗的被子*

**Dr. Art School of Expressive Arts & Therapy**
香港藝術心理會

# 3-5911 Cooney Road, Richmond
BC V6X4H2  Canada
www.seedrart.com
szeoi@yahoo.com